Joseph E. Davis, Pioneer Patriarch

JOSEPH E. DAVIS

PIONEER PATRIARCH

Janet Sharp Hermann

UNIVERSITY PRESS OF MISSISSIPPI
Jackson & London

Copyright © 1990 by University Press of Mississippi
All rights reserved
Manufactured in the United States of America
94 93 92 91   4 3 2 1

The paper in this book meets the guidelines for permanence and
durability of the Committee on Production Guidelines for Book
Longevity of the Council on Library Resources.

Library of Congress Cataloging-in-Publication Data

Hermann, Janet Sharp.
   Joseph E. Davis : pioneer patriarch / Janet Sharp Hermann.
      p.   cm.
   Includes bibliographical references and index.
   ISBN 0-87805-488-x (alk. paper)
      1. Davis, Joseph E., d. 1870   2. Davis, Jefferson, 1808–1889—
Family.   3. Plantation owners—Mississippi—Biography.
4. Plantation life—Mississippi—History—19th century.
5. Mississippi—Biography.   6. Davis family.   I. Title.
F341.D25H47   1990
976.2′00992—dc20
[B]   90-49293
                                                         CIP

British Library Cataloging-in-Publication data available

FOR BILL

who taught me about men

CONTENTS

PREFACE

THIS IS THE LIFE STORY of a wealthy cotton planter in ante-bellum Mississippi. Joseph E. Davis did not own the largest plantation or the greatest number of slaves in the state, although he was among the top ten. He was not a prominent statesman, holding only two minor public offices, although for some years he exercised considerable influence in the Democratic party. His name does not appear in most annals of American or even southern history. And yet there are a number of reasons why his life merits close study.

Most obvious is that Jefferson Davis, the president of the Confederacy, was his youngest brother. This relationship first called Joseph Davis to my attention, but in retrospect it proved to be among the least important facets of his story. Certainly this close family bond—theirs was almost a father-son relationship—gave Joseph more intimate contact with the national political scene than most planters had. Many contemporary observers noted the importance of Joseph's influence on his famous younger brother. This might entitle him to a minor place in Confederate history.

But as I delved into it, Joseph Davis's life became fascinating on its own merits. He was a man on the move, both physically and intellectually, in true American style. Born on the Georgia frontier at the close of the American Revolution, which had touched both his parents, Davis grew to manhood opening up new lands in Kentucky. With independent study and an avid thirst for knowledge he rose to the top of the law profession while helping shape the new state of Mississippi. Then with his considerable earnings and entrepreneurial skill he built a model plantation, demonstrating scientific agriculture and innovative slave management techniques. His is a quintessentially American success story.

I discovered that Joseph Davis's life provides a marvelous window through which to view intimately almost a century of American history. He experienced most of the major events of his time from the Revolution and the War of 1812 through the Civil War. The Second Great Awakening began in his neighborhood, and he was in the Mississippi Valley during the New Madrid earthquake of 1811–12 and when the first steamboat chugged down the river. He encountered most of the prominent people of that century from George Washington, Andrew Jackson, John C. Calhoun, Zachary Taylor, and Andrew Johnson to all leading Mississippi and Confederate politicians and generals.

Joseph Davis could not be called a typical cotton planter. It is true that he displayed some of the characteristics of planters labeled "paternalistic" by James Oakes and Eugene Genovese; certainly he fostered a patriarchal, extended household which included whites and slaves alike. But Davis differed profoundly from the Oakes-Genovese model in his attitude toward his slaves. Never doubting their inherent humanity, he allowed them to develop their individual skills and to enjoy the resulting economic benefits. Perhaps as a result of his wide travels and reading, he held many ideas more prevalent in the North such as a dedication to free market commercialism and liberal democracy. Unlike the stereotype, he was not aristocratic by birth nor did he pretend to be. The prime driving force in his life was his warm affection for his large family.

Throughout this work I have asked myself how the world appeared to Joseph Davis from where he stood at that particular time. What was it like to hear Indians and wild animals call through the night in up-country Georgia? To trudge the rough trail through the Cumberland Gap? To travel the circuit in the wake of a judge in rural Kentucky? To jounce along back roads in a stagecoach or navigate the Mississippi aboard a luxurious steamboat? To go from a frontier cabin to an elegant mansion, then back to a makeshift refugee hovel? In every case I have tried to recapture the feel and texture of his time and place. This seems to me the real excitement of history.

This book has benefited from the generous assistance of able staff members at many institutions, especially the Library of Congress and the National Archives in Washington, the Mississippi Department of Archives and History in Jackson, and numerous university libraries. Several kind individuals have shared family documents with me, including Frances Porter of San Francisco and Judie DaCostello of Reno.

Illustrations have been made possible through the cooperation of Gordon Cotton at the Old Courthouse Museum in Vicksburg; Cory Hudgins of the Museum of the Confederacy in Richmond; Lise Lorber, a direct descendant of Joseph Davis, from New Orleans; and Ernesto Caldeira, who provided copies of the marvelous oil portraits at Rosemont Plantation.

I have profited immeasurably from the continuing thoughtfulness and friendship of Lynda Crist and Mary Dix, editors of the Papers of Jefferson Davis at Rice University. The late Frank E. Everett, Jr., of Vicksburg was an inspiration and help to me from the beginning; I only wish he could have lived to see the final work. I am also grateful to Seetha Srinivasan, associate director and editor-in-chief of the University Press of Mississippi, for her astute editorial advice.

Finally I want to thank my family for their active cooperation. My daughter Kristina Stevens painstakingly read and criticized the original manuscript and my son William, Jr., cheerfully contributed his many practical skills. My greatest debt is to my husband William D. Hermann who has always warmly encouraged my work; he made possible this book that is lovingly dedicated to him.

Joseph E. Davis, Pioneer Patriarch

ONE

Frontier Heritage

WHEN JOSEPH EMORY DAVIS WAS BORN on December 10, 1784, Wilkes County, Georgia, was only beginning to recover from the death and destruction that had swept the Carolina-Georgia frontier during the American Revolution. The pioneer population was almost evenly divided between Whigs and Tories, pitting neighbor against neighbor in a bitter civil war across the sparsely settled territory. Joseph's father, Samuel Davis, and his two half-brothers had joined the rebel militia, leaving their widowed mother alone on the farm. After a foray into East Florida, Samuel was wounded only a few miles from the Davis farm at the famous Battle of Kettle Creek. Later, he led a company at the sieges of Savannah and Augusta which finally cleared British forces from the colony of Georgia by mid-1782.[1]

During one of his sorties across the Savannah River into South Carolina, Samuel Davis had met the charming Jane Cook; they were married in July 1783. The state of Georgia granted land generously to veterans of the recent conflict as well as to new arrivals so the young couple immediately began clearing a

3

farm on two hundred acres beside the Little River in southern Wilkes County. During the next two years the Davises acquired a total of some nineteen hundred acres of land in Wilkes and Washington counties in Georgia and another two thousand acres in South Carolina. Even though land was so plentiful that it had little immediate value, the ownership and development of real property was considered the passport to wealth in the new nation. The future looked promising for the young Davis family when Joseph was born.[2]

During the first few years after Joseph's birth, there was renewed trouble between Indians and settlers on the Georgia frontier. Although with the departure of the British, the Cherokees left that land to the development of aggressive whites, the Creeks refused to abide by treaties that deprived them of the rich area west of the Oconee River. It was commonplace for settlers to lose cattle or the few slaves they owned to roving bands of Creeks, but there were more ominous developments during the fall before Joseph's third birthday. In a three-month period, thirty-one whites were killed and the new village of Greensborough only a few miles to the west was destroyed by Indians seeking to preserve their land. The previous August Samuel Davis had paid his half-brother Isaac Williams one hundred pounds in hard-earned specie for 575 acres on Town Creek to the west near the Oconee; now sporadic Indian warfare made it unsafe to develop the land. Eventually, through the intervention of the federal government, the Creeks were induced to sign a treaty designed to bring peace to the Oconee lands. But Joseph Davis grew up in a society of wary farmers who watched wandering Indians with suspicion. Even the reassuring visit of the revered war hero and new president, George Washington, to Wilkes County in 1791 failed to convince the settlers that their homesteads were indeed secure.[3]

Responsible citizens quickly organized local government agencies to ensure orderly enforcement of the law on the new frontier. They were equally anxious to provide education for their children. The Georgia statute providing for the establishment of the town of Washington as the Wilkes County seat and the erection of a courthouse there also mandated the establishment of a free academy, but the classes that began in the new building in 1786 were continued for only two years. Since Joseph Davis was just four years old when this, the only formal school in his area, ceased operations, his education was acquired in a more casual fashion.

Both Samuel and Jane Davis were literate—a considerable accomplishment for young people who had grown up on the Carolina-Georgia frontier during the Revolution, when education of any kind was rare. Fewer than one-third of those who left wills in Wilkes County in this period could write, and the rate of illiteracy must have been even higher among those who died intestate. Learning his letters from his parents, young Joseph received enough instruction to develop a thirst for knowledge that led him to a lifetime of self-education. Like his contemporary John C. Calhoun, who grew up just across the Savannah River in Ninety-Six District, South Carolina, Joseph Davis was largely self-taught. The isolated early life of these lads provided much opportunity for reflection and fostered an independence of mind that served them well in later life.[4]

When Joseph was six months old, his father joined with other like-minded settlers in the area to form the Phillips Mill Baptist Church and build a log chapel. Christian tolerance came slowly to the battle-scarred congregation, however; old Tories were not welcome at the services. Although born after the Revolution, young Joseph Davis learned to hate former British loyalists along with his Bible lessons.[5]

Early conditioning may have given Davis a feeling of fear and loathing for the Indian, but his attitude toward blacks was probably just the opposite. By the time he was three, the Davis family had acquired at least one slave, a woman named Winny, as partial payment for a valuable plot of land that Samuel Davis sold to Stephen Gafford, a prosperous neighbor and fellow church member. Since slaves represented a large capital investment and young males sold for about fifty pounds and females for some thirty pounds, few frontiersmen could afford more than one or two. Until 1800 no resident of Wilkes County held more than thirty slaves, and the majority of householders owned none. Winny must have been a welcome addition to the Davis menage, sharing with Jane the care of three-year-old Joseph and baby Benjamin as well as the endless tasks required to provide food and clothing for all. The three new babies that arrived in the next four years made Winny's services ever more appreciated, and as a tot Joseph probably regarded her as a source of both comfort and authority second only to his parents. It is interesting that although Jane Davis never joined the Phillips Mill Baptist Church, the slave Winny was a member and, along with Samuel Davis, formally withdrew her letter from it when the family prepared to leave the state.

The position of black members in the Phillips Mill Baptist Church reflects the attitude of that eighteenth-century rural society toward the race. Although each new member was listed as "Turner's Sam" or "Chiver's Amy" or "Samuel Davis's Winny," he or she seemed to suffer no restriction in worship. Not until September 1791, after the Davises had withdrawn their membership, did the congregation mandate segregated seating. Although more than one-third of the members were slaves, they were not cited by church officials for alleged misconduct as often as were the white members. The leaders of the frontier church recognized that slaves were not in complete control of their lives and perhaps should not be held to as strict moral standards as the whites, but they were uncertain about where to fix the limits. But church leaders never suggested that emancipation was the proper solution. Only one Wilkes County resident is known to have taken this path; Donald Grant, an active

Methodist and prosperous landholder in the Little River neighborhood, provided in his will for the gradual freeing of his slaves when the males reached age thirty-one and the females twenty-eight.[6]

Discrimination based on the concept of racial inferiority was only beginning to appear in the Wilkes County of Joseph Davis's boyhood. His father had fought beside the mulatto Austin Dabney at the Battle of Kettle Creek and witnessed the act of heroism that saved their leader, Elijah Clark, and cost Dabney a dangerous wound. The white Harris family nursed the respected black soldier back to health and then lived with him on his veteran's land grant for many years. Of course, Austin Dabney's acceptance in Wilkes County was based on his willingness to maintain a modest, unassertive manner and to sacrifice any thought of a wife and family of his own so he could provide for the care and education of the young Harris son.

In the early 1790s a small number of white refugees from the black revolution in Santo Domingo settled in Wilkes County bringing hair-raising tales of slave atrocities on their West Indian island, but their racial fears must have seemed exaggerated in predominantly white up-country Georgia. Many settlers who had fought for the ideas embodied in the Declaration of Independence probably agreed in principle with Donald Grant when he stated in his will that he was "fully convinced that perpetual slavery is unjust and contrary to the natural rights of all mankind." But no others carried these convictions to their logical conclusion by emancipating the few bondsmen they held. Nevertheless, a boy growing up on that labor-short frontier would have considered the slaves he knew as worthy members of the community.[7]

By 1793 Samuel Davis had decided to move his growing family to a more promising region. Tobacco had exhausted the poorer soil in parts of Wilkes County, and in the ten years since the termination of hostilities Davis had not achieved the prosperity enjoyed by some of his neighbors who owned more slaves. Displaying the restlessness typical of frontiersmen, as well as the optimism that made the newest area open to settlement seem irresistibly promising, the Davises packed their possessions and headed for a new frontier.

The family went first to South Carolina, where Jane's relatives and friends were enthusiastic about the possibility of emigrating across the mountains to Kentucky. The Hardins, a family from that community who had made the trek more than a decade earlier, had sent back eyewitness reports of opportunities that were becoming ever more attractive. Kentucky had been admitted to the Union in 1792 with a constitution that allowed all free white males over twenty-one to vote with no religious or property qualifications. This transmontane district had been a bloody battleground during the Revolution, when British-backed Shawnee and Wyandotte tribes had decimated the small white population. At war's end, however, the new United States government undertook to defeat the Indians decisively and confiscate their lands. This ruthless policy brought some measure of peace to Kentucky. The Davises were accustomed to dealing with occasional small bands of Native Americans and were not discouraged by tales of isolated raids along the paths to the new land. When Jane and Samuel learned that Jane's sister and her husband, William Pitchford, had decided to make the journey, the Davises joined the caravan.[8]

To reach Kentucky the party followed the Cherokee Path and other Indian trails that carried them through the Carolinas northeast of the Blue Ridge Mountains. Then they made the arduous trek westward through the Cumberland Gap on a rugged trail too narrow to accommodate wagons. The nine-year-old Joseph Davis was unlikely to forget that hundred-mile month-long ordeal.[9]

Unfortunately for those who braved the rigors of migration to Kentucky, by the mid-1790s most of the rich land in the Blue

Grass region had already been claimed and was selling for as much as $100 per acre. Like many others, the Davises were forced to move on, settling in Mercer County in the center of the state, where they could raise livestock on rented land. There was a constant demand for both cattle and horses among the prosperous Blue Grass planters, and soon surplus Kentucky animals were being driven back over the Wilderness Road to larger markets in Philadelphia, Baltimore, Richmond, and Charleston. Samuel Davis did well; by May 1795 he owned six horses and fifteen cattle, and his herd increased the next year. But he owned no land so after less than three years in Mercer County the family began making plans to move farther west into newer regions recently opened to settlement.

After considerable consultation and some exploratory trips, Samuel Davis and his brother-in-law William Pitchford decided to take their families into the Green River country of west-central Kentucky. This river flows west and then north for some 370 miles, draining almost a quarter of the state as well as a portion of northern Tennessee. The land south and west of Green River had been opened to veterans' claims even before Kentucky separated from Virginia in 1792, and the new state continued to encourage settlement in the region. In 1795 the Kentucky legislature ruled that settlers living on unclaimed land in the Green River area could buy two hundred acres for the low price of only $60. With these inducements, in the fall of 1796 Davis and Pitchford sold most of their livestock, packed their meager household goods on the remaining horses, and again took to the trail.[10]

When they reached Barren County, the Pitchfords turned south to the plot of land they had chosen, not far from the Tennessee border in an area that later became Allen County. The Davis family continued west to a region slated to become Warren County on January first. Here Stephen Hardin, Jane's kinsman and one of the early pioneers from Ninety-Six in South

Carolina, sold them half the headright he had claimed some years before. Earlier in the year Samuel had visited the area, surveyed the hundred-acre plot, and found it to his liking. To pay for his farm Davis sold the last of his cattle and all but one horse, but he retained the two adult slaves.[11]

Here in Warren County, Kentucky, Joseph Davis spent the years from age twelve to sixteen helping his father and the male slave with the many tasks required to carve out a viable farm from virgin wilderness. Raising the all-important corn and hogs as well as some cattle and horses, the Davises were a typical hardworking pioneer family. In 1797, a year after settling in the new home, Jane Davis gave birth to a daughter, the first baby in five years, to be followed by four others over the next decade. As the oldest child, Joseph was responsible for supervision of the younger ones, especially the older four who had been born in Georgia. As well as helping on the farm, a frontier lad was expected to become a skilled woodsman who contributed fish, game, and wild fruit to the family table.

The Green River country seemed to attract dangerous outlaws along with other settlers. To protect the community, aroused citizens sometimes resorted to extralegal measures, including lynching of accused criminals. Concerned leaders sought a solution to the problem of criminality and immorality by establishing churches. Soon scattered congregations of Christian worshipers of various denominations dotted the Cumberland region of Kentucky north of the Tennessee border. The settlers' desire to purify their society made this area the seedbed of the emotional revival movement known as the Second Great Awakening. It swept first Kentucky and Tennessee, then engulfed the remaining frontier and much of the nation.[12]

By the summer of 1800, as the revival movement gained momentum in their old neighborhood, the Davis family had once more moved farther west. This time Samuel Davis chose a plot of land directly on a waterway, the West Fork of the Red River;

perhaps he had found the Warren County place too inconvenient because it lacked access by boat. The new farm was west of Russellville just over the border from Logan County in an area that had been designated Christian County on January 1, 1797. Soon the Davises were settled on two hundred acres of land that Samuel had surveyed himself, and he and his two slaves and all available children were repeating the familiar process of clearing and planting new fields.[13]

From the beginning things seemed to go well for the Davises in the rolling green hills of Christian County. In November 1800, Samuel and Jane sold the one-hundred-acre Warren County farm for the substantial sum of one hundred pounds; Samuel carefully recorded the sale along with his wife's relinquishment of her dower rights in the records of both Warren and Christian counties. Supplementing his income by serving as county surveyor, Davis was able to buy another adult slave in 1801 and three more horses the next year. By this time the Davis family had built a comfortable double log cabin which contained two large rooms on either side of a covered passage, each with its fireplace and attached small shed room. The puncheon floors, small-paned windows, and doors hung on wooden hinges and fastened with wooden buttons marked this as the snug home of a prosperous farm family. To contribute further to the family's prosperity, they procured a tavern license and for the next two years took in the wayfarers who frequented the road from Russellville to Hopkinsville, the tiny new Christian County seat. The Davises received small compensation for lodging because, according to the rates fixed by the Logan County Court in 1801, a tavernkeeper could charge only six cents for that service. Their profit must have come from the food and especially the drink they served.[14]

The problems and pleasures of keeping a public house had little effect on young Joseph Davis because Samuel and Jane decided soon after moving to Christian County that it was time for their eldest to learn a trade. He knew all about frontier farming, but even if that were to be his chosen career he must go out into the world and earn enough money to buy his own land; with Samuel's growing family and limited resources, Joseph would be unlikely to inherit a sizable estate. So in 1801 the sixteen-year-old lad was apprenticed to a merchant in the burgeoning town of Russellville.

Even in such a remote area of the frontier the general store carried an amazing variety of goods from faraway places. It would stock sugar and spices, coffee, various kinds of tea, and imported brandy, sherry, and port. In addition to gunpowder and salt, the Russellville store of Stewart, Dromgoole and Company carried a wide variety of fabrics for those who could afford clothes and bedding made from something finer than linsey-woolsey or other homespun cloth. In November 1806 the store offered "Rose and Point Blankets, Red, Yellow and White Flannels, Coatings, Coarse and Fine Broad Cloths, Cassimers, Velvets, Thicksets, Bennet's Constitution and Fancy Cords" besides the usual "Linnens [sic], Callicoes, &c., &c."[15]

The clerk's job included more than merely measuring out proper quantities of dry goods and food. Accepting payment was a tricky task where there was no standard monetary system. Accounts were sometimes kept in dollars but just as often in shillings and pence. Payments were made in coins from European countries along with some from India and the Middle East, and their worth had to be fixed by weight with the Spanish piaster serving as the standard of value. The few bank notes that circulated were not trusted as much as the tobacco warehouse receipts or land warrants issued by the state treasurer. But most people lacked any of these resources and resorted to payment in kind. The Russellville store announced that it would give a good exchange for "Cotton, Whiskey, Tallow, Beeswax, and Hogs-lard" but undoubtedly also accepted tobacco, pelts, salt, gunpowder, lead, and most anything else that could be resold either in Logan County or in the markets of Natchez and New Orleans. Local merchants were often forced to act as bankers and extend credit, sometimes using the notes as a circulating medium. The complex operations of such a rural trading center gave young Davis a grasp of business functions that proved useful throughout his adult life.[16]

With money saved from his years as a clerk, Joseph was able to buy four hundred acres of good land in the vicinity of his parents' farm on the Red River. When he was twenty-one the land could be registered in his own name, although for tax purposes it was still lumped together with that of his family, making a total of eleven hundred acres owned by the Davis family. Joseph did not plan a career either as a full-time farmer or a storekeeper. Instead, by 1805 he had decided to emulate some of the most prosperous men he knew and return to Russellville to read law.[17]

The legal profession provided an excellent opportunity for an ambitious young man on the Kentucky frontier because of the frequency of conflicting land claims. There were a number of causes for such actions. A shortage of trained surveyors resulted in a dearth of systematic land surveys. Complex and sometimes contradictory land laws from Virginia and Kentucky, vague grants to soldiers, and bogus sales by unscrupulous speculators resulted in a plethora of overlapping claims. Squatters' insistence on their rights to their farms added to the general litigiousness. The French traveler François Michaux found more concern about establishing clear titles to their land among Kentuckians than in any other state he visited. He noted, "I never stopped at the house of a single inhabitant, who did not appear convinced of the validity of his own title, while he doubted that of his neighbor." This attitude led to thousands of lawsuits furnishing employment for an army of lawyers who crossed the mountains and floated down the rivers close on the heels of the pioneers.[18]

Twenty years earlier another ambitious young man, Andrew Jackson, had recognized the advantages of reading law and by 1805 had established a flourishing practice in Nashville, Tennessee, just a short distance south of the Davis farm. Despite this propinquity, there is no evidence that Joseph Davis knew enough about Jackson at this time to use him as a model. It is far more likely that he had been swayed by observing close at hand men such as Ninian Edwards, who arrived in Russellville in 1798 with little but his law certificate. Within five years he had not only built up a vigorous practice but also had accumulated substantial landholdings in addition to a tanyard and a distillery. Edwards was named judge of the general court in 1802, became a circuit judge two years later, and was advanced to the court of appeals in 1806. No wonder Davis chose this popular avenue to wealth and success.[19]

Although the population of Russellville totaled less than three hundred, there were several lawyers with whom Davis could have studied. He selected William Wallace, who came to Logan County from Maryland in 1791 and began buying property, accumulating more than fourteen hundred acres by 1806. Among his holdings was a one-hundred-acre plot on the west fork of the Red River in the vicinity of the Davis farm. Wallace entered the legal profession later in life and was not admitted to the bar until 1802, so when Davis joined him three years later he was scarcely a veteran lawyer. His reputation grew rapidly, however, and in 1807 he was named to fill the vacancy on the circuit court left by the advancement of Ninian Edwards to the court of appeals. Wallace, who became a close friend and adviser to young Davis, was a tall, fair-haired man of great intelligence. His manner was taciturn and quiet in a profession known for its flamboyant loquaciousness. Wallace was a committed Jeffersonian Republican, who announced that as a presidential elector in 1808 he would cast his vote for James Madison. Samuel Davis, like many of his neighbors, had been a Whig against the Tories and was now a Republican against Federalists; as he came to understand the issues, Joseph Davis wholeheartedly concurred with the views of his father and his mentor.[20]

Wallace's jurisdiction covered five counties some 160 miles in extent. Trekking through the woods accompanied by a coterie of lawyers, he usually covered the distances with his rifle over his shoulder and was reputed to be an excellent shot. While traveling with him, his apprentices developed their marksmanship along with their legal knowledge. Three times a year the judge held court for a week or two in each county, joined on the bench by two nonprofessional local assistant judges. When court was in session, the county seats were bustling places, with farmers coming in to attend court, engage in trade, and enjoy the social opportunities. Undoubtedly the young law students combined considerable recreation with their legal duties. At times, the overcrowded taverns took on the atmosphere of an Elks convention, with noisy high-jinks and practical jokes.[21]

Back in Russellville, life had its exciting moments even when court was not in session. This dynamic little town was growing rapidly, climbing from fourteenth in size in the state in 1800 to eighth a decade later. It was the primary business center for southwestern Kentucky, attracting an increasing number of industries in addition to trading ventures. As a handsome young man in his early twenties, Joseph Davis undoubtedly led a busy social life, attending many informal gatherings as well as the rather pretentious celebrations of important occasions. For example, on July 4, 1807, he was one of the guests at a dinner given by the Russellville Volunteers at which there was much food, "an abundance of good wine," and many toasts to the great nation and its national and local leaders. Although no women were invited to the banquet, afterward many of the guests retired to Captain Ninian Edwards's house, where they joined "a brilliant circle of ladies." Though he avoided the marital tie that entangled most young men of his age, during these years Davis developed social skills that made him a favorite with women throughout his life.[22]

As Joseph Davis completed his legal studies, his father began selling his land. By 1809 he had converted the eleven-hundred-acre farm in Christian County into fourteen horses and four slaves in preparation for another move. Persistent dissatisfaction with his economic situation and recurrent hope of better luck in a new location were probably the primary motives for this as for earlier moves. The year before, the aging parents welcomed their tenth and last child, whom they named Jefferson. Even though the two oldest sons did not live at home, this large family was a heavy responsibility for a man whose business ability never quite measured up to his needs.[23]

One reason for the Davis family's decision to leave the area may have been Joseph's involvement with the respected Shelby family. In November 1808 unwed sixteen-year-old Rachel Shelby gave birth to a son, whom she named William Davis; apparently Joseph Davis was the father. Davis's failure to marry Rachel no doubt caused a major scandal in the community and a bitter rift between the two noted families. In any case, within two years both had left Kentucky: the Shelbys for Illinois and the Davises first for Louisiana and then Mississippi. There is no evidence that Davis contributed to the support of Rachel or their son. More than fifty years later, after Joseph's death, his brother Jefferson acknowledged the family's obligations by offering William Davis a plot of land if he would move to Mississippi; William, by then a prosperous Illinois farmer, declined.[24]

In 1810 Samuel Davis and his family made the long trek down the Natchez Trace from Nashville some six hundred miles south to their destination, a farm on Bayou Teche in southern Louisiana. After an unhappy year in this swampy area, where mosquitoes were a constant nuisance and the younger children were always sick, they moved again. This time they traveled only some ninety miles to what proved to be their permanent home, a small farm in Wilkinson County, Mississippi Territory. Joseph Davis was so pleased with the area that he made arrangements to read law in the nearby town of Pinckneyville.[25]

Thus in 1811, at the age of twenty-six, Joseph Davis left the developing region of western Kentucky for another frontier. He had spent his formative years growing up with the society of the Green River area, and he retained many friends there. He always cherished a fondness for Kentucky and a respect for its intellectual climate; in later years he sent numerous relatives and wards to its schools. But he had determined to cast his lot with a newer land, partly so that he could be close to his large family for whom he always felt a great responsibility. Recognizing his father's lack of business competence, Joseph willingly shouldered some of the burden of providing for his siblings. Beyond that, the young lawyer would have a hand in building a new state, for it was clear that the Mississippi Territory would eventually enter the Union. Although he might have had a legal career in Russellville, Davis opted for the newer land. For him, Kentucky was already a part of the old, established past.

TWO

Founding a State and a Fortune

EIGHTEEN ELEVEN, the year Joseph Davis moved from the newly settled state of Kentucky to the raw frontier of Mississippi Territory, was an extraordinary time. The federal government was moving closer to war with Britain over its disregard for the United States's neutral rights. The trade embargo imposed by President Thomas Jefferson had crippled the American economy without significantly damaging the enemy. The nation was bitterly divided over the advisability of going to war with England; the merchants of the Northeast feared that further interference with trade would mean more idle ships and unsold goods. In contrast, citizens of the newer regions of the Southwest believed a successful war would stop the British from illegally arming and inciting the Indians as they had seemed to do so effectively since the close of the Revolution a generation earlier. General William Henry Harrison's November victory over the British-backed Indians at Tippecanoe in Indiana Territory fed the rampantly nationalistic spirit among settlers in the West. They demanded the defeat and expulsion of the British, preferably from the entire continent, thus allowing the United States to annex Canada and the Floridas. Mississippians were growing impatient with the intransigence of the British and the indecision of the federal government.

During the year 1811, however, residents of the Mississippi Valley were more alarmed by acts of nature than by those of hostile nations. Spring planting was disrupted by heavy flooding, which inundated many newly cleared fields near the river and its tributaries. The high water also impeded traffic on streams that were often the only trade routes for the region. More frightening, if less damaging, in September a large and very bright comet with a long, forked tail appeared, lending an eerie glow to the night sky until well into the new year. While the scientific community speculated on the potential danger of the earth's collision with this strange body, pious common folk worried about the wrath of God and Indians sought protection from their shamen.

By the time the comet lighted up the September night, Joseph Davis was probably established in the little settlement of Pinckneyville in Wilkinson County, where he read law with Joseph Johnson, a Virginian, who had become a prosperous lawyer-planter in Mississippi. Two years earlier a visitor had described Pinckneyville as "a straggling village of ten houses, mostly in decay, and some of them uninhabited . . . [containing] a little church, a tavern, a store and a post-office." It was only a mile and a half from the border of that part of West Florida recently incorporated into Orleans Territory. The change resulted from a bloodless rebellion against Spain by the Yankees, who constituted most of the population there. Joseph Davis apparently remained in this unpromising setting only until the end of the year while he acquired enough knowledge of local law to apply for admission to the Mississippi bar.[1]

About the time Davis took his new legal learning north to the territorial capital of Washington, six miles east of Natchez on the Trace, nature again reminded the pioneers of their insignificance and mortality. In the predawn hours of December 16, 1811, people up and down the midcontinent were jolted awake by the first shock of the most severe earthquake to strike North America in recorded history. The epicenter was in the middle Mississippi Valley at New Madrid in Missouri Territory, but this and two subsequent shocks in January and February were felt over an area of 1 million square miles. The quakes rang church bells, stopped pendulum clocks, moved furniture, and cracked pavements and plaster as far east as Charleston, South Carolina, and Norfolk and Richmond, Virginia. Residents in Detroit and across the border in Canada some six hundred miles from the epicenter counted nine sharp shocks in the next three months, and an engineer in Louisville less that two hundred miles from New Madrid recorded 1,874 tremors of varying intensity in that time. Joseph Davis in the lower Mississippi Valley certainly felt the earth shake. Modern seismologists have estimated that each of the three major tremors was more intense than the devastating San Francisco earthquake of 1906.

Despite the severity of the 1811–12 quakes, their epicenter was so sparsely populated that only a dozen deaths were recorded. The psychological trauma, however, drove many who had spent little time in church suddenly to embrace religion. From impromptu prayer meetings as the earth shook to well-organized camp meetings that spring and summer, the people joined in pious practices in unprecedented numbers. But preachers who hailed the disaster as God's way of strengthening the church were disappointed in subsequent months when these new converts, dubbed "earthquake Christians," quickly returned to their careless ways.[2]

On December 20, 1811, four days after the first earthquake, the first steamboat to navigate the Mississippi docked in Natchez inaugurating a new era in transportation that would greatly enhance the prosperity of the region. Since the boat was traveling on down the river to New Orleans, a prosperous cotton planter who happened to be named Samuel Davis decided to risk sending a bale of cotton on this experimental voyage. Little did Joseph Davis dream at the time that his future life would be closely tied to the commerce begun by a stranger who shared his father's name.[3]

Far more significant for Davis's immediate goals, on January 16, 1812, Governor David Holmes appointed him an attorney at law for Mississippi Territory. In the course of his travels to and from Kentucky, Davis had sought out promising places to establish his law practice; he now proceeded to move to his choice, Greenville in Jefferson County. This town, located twenty-four miles east of Natchez, was one of the largest on the Natchez Trace. Until 1809 there had been intense rivalry between Greenville, the center of the Republican planter faction, and the older city of Natchez with its satellite, Washington, where Federalist influence had prevailed. Under the soothing administration of Governor Holmes, whom President Jefferson had appointed to calm the factional strife, and with the rise of more crucial national and international problems, petty local rivalries gave way to greater unity among the frontier settlements.

An early traveler found old Greenville "very handsomely situated, on a dry sandy plain near the middle branch of Cole's Creek. It is surrounded at a little distance by small farms and woods, which add variety and beauty to its appearance." The half-mile-long main street was intersected by two smaller cross streets "containing in all forty tolerably good houses." Among prominent buildings were the small courthouse, a jail with pillory, a post office, and an interdenominational church. Commerce was limited to two stores, two taverns, and an apothecary's shop. Unlike the towns nearer the river, Greenville had no marshlands nearby to breed malaria-carrying mosquitoes. But it suffered from another disadvantage. After every heavy rain Cole's Creek flooded, temporarily isolating the town. Perhaps this inconvenience was outweighed in Joseph Davis's view by the number of wealthy people who lived on prosperous estates in the surrounding countryside. Prominent men such as Cato West, Cowles Mead, Thomas Hinds, and Governor Holmes all lived within two miles of Greenville and promised to provide the sort of clients a young lawyer sought. By September 1812, nine months after his arrival, Davis had become so well established that Governor Holmes honored him with an appointment as justice of the peace for Jefferson County.[4]

By the summer of 1813 conditions in Mississippi Territory looked less promising to the eager new settlers for a number of reasons, both internal and external. Most newcomers were in debt for their lands and therefore heavily dependent on the proceeds of each crop, but in many cases spring floods had reduced yields. Incomes were further diminished by the international situation. Angered over its inability to gain recognition of neutral rights, the United States had finally declared war on England in June 1812. Most Mississippians were as eager as other Americans for their young nation to defend its rights against their former British oppressors. Within a year, however, economic damage was apparent even in the remote settlements of Mississippi. The falling price of cotton, increased costs for goods they must buy, and higher wartime taxes further reduced settlers' incomes. In November, Governor David Holmes mobilized small companies of militia from most counties in the territory and sent them to Baton Rouge for six months' service in the United States Army. In April 1813, when the important port of Mobile was seized by General James Wilkinson and incorporated within the Mississippi Territory, the greatest danger to the region was thought to come from British naval operations along the Gulf coast.[5]

Within a few months it became apparent that unrest among the Creek Indians in the eastern part of the territory posed a greater threat than the British. This tribe was backed by the

British and incited by the charismatic Tecumseh and his fol-
lowers from the North, who sought to unite the Indians for a
desperate effort to preserve their lands from white incursions. A
militant group of Creeks, called the Red Sticks, decided to make
war on white settlements in the Mississippi Territory despite
opposition within their own tribe. Rumors of ritualistic preparations for battle spread quickly through the exposed commu-
nities on the eastern frontier of the territory. When in late July a
band of painted warriors was sighted on the trail to Pensacola, it
was assumed that they were planning an attack. A handful of
militiamen reinforced by volunteers hastily gathered at a frontier fort and set out to intercept the Creeks. At a spring on Burnt
Corn Creek they found the weary Indians and mounted a sur-
prise attack that drove them into the canebrake in disarray. The
Creeks quickly rallied, and when they saw the small group of
whites inattentively looting their camp, they launched a counter-
attack that routed the raw militiamen.

The war party of Creeks, infuriated by this unprovoked attack by the frontiersmen, determined on revenge. On August 30
they attacked Fort Mims, north of Mobile, a recently erected
frontier stockade, where many of the gathered settlers were
celebrating the arrival of a supply of whiskey instead of watching for attackers. After several hours of brutal fighting, the fort
fell; of some five hundred whites, including women and children, only about fifty survived either as prisoners or fugitives
hiding in the woods.[6]

News of the Fort Mims massacre aroused fear throughout the
Mississippi Territory. On September 11 Governor Holmes called
for mobilization of additional troops, including a cavalry force
under the direction of Major Thomas Hinds. The ranks of these
Mississippi dragoons were quickly filled by young men in the
river counties who could provide themselves with horses for
what many viewed as a grand adventure. Among those from
Jefferson County who rallied to the call to arms was Joseph E.

Davis, attorney and justice of the peace. On September 13, just two days after the governor issued his draft call, Davis and his younger brother Samuel joined Captain Doherty's company at Washington. As privates they were each entitled to eight dollars a month plus forty cents per day for hire and risk of the horse. Nine days later, these dragoons were sent to Fort Stoddert on the eastern frontier near the junction of the Alabama and Tombigbee rivers. That same day the Davis brothers transferred to the cavalry company from Adams County headed by Captain James Kempe. Although there is no record of their reasons for making this change, they may have had close friends in the new company, or Joseph may have thought it would be more advantageous for his later career to get acquainted with men from Natchez, the metropolis of the territory. One result of the transfer was Joseph's acquaintance with James Kempe, whose daughter Margaret later married his best friend and whose granddaughter was to become his sister-in-law some forty years hence.[7]

The Mississippi militia under General Ferdinand L. Claiborne was mustered into the United States service and assigned to General Thomas Flournoy, commander of the Seventh District headquartered in Mobile. He promptly sent the dragoons to protect the settlers along the Tombigbee, who were trying to harvest their crops despite the Indian menace. The Creeks hid in the heavily timbered swamps from which small groups of warriors suddenly emerged to pick off militia scouts or settlers in lonely clearings. The cavalry's task of searching for these illusive braves and guarding isolated cabins and corn fields seemed dull and unmilitary to the venturesome young men of Hinds's command who had enlisted to win glory in battle. Individualistic frontiersmen that they were, they drafted a letter to General Flournoy candidly stating their discontent and demanding that they be allowed to attack Creek strongholds farther inland. The commander, who tended to underestimate the seriousness of the Indian menace, was determined to keep his troops near the coast to ward off a possible British attack on Mobile. Resenting any criticism of his policies, Flournoy was so angered by the cavalrymen's letter that he returned these Mississippi dragoons to Governor Holmes for alleged insubordination.

Thus Joseph Davis's military career lasted just over two months. He and his brother were mustered out when the Adams Troop disbanded in the capital of the territory on November 24, 1813. This brief taste of life in the army was enough for Davis; even though a military career was regarded as an acceptable means of upward mobility for an ambitious southerner and Davis made it possible for his youngest brother to follow this path, he never chose it for himself. He probably found the regimentation unpalatable. His experiences as a pioneer on three frontiers had taught him to value freedom of choice, and he took orders reluctantly. Now that he had attained the position of attorney, he could achieve his goal of material success without subordinating himself to any superior officer. He held to this commitment in spite of heavy counterpressures. For example, the next year, when patriotism was running high, his brothers Samuel and Isaac joined Colonel Hinds and his cavalrymen in their march to New Orleans. There they won the praise of their commander, General Andrew Jackson, but Joseph remained in Greenville pursuing his career in the law.[8]

The end of the War of 1812 ushered in a period of unprecedented growth for Mississippi Territory. The defeat of the Creek Indians opened more than 20 million additional acres to settlement. At the same time, after Jackson's victory at New Orleans opened the Mississippi River to commerce and assured America's access to world markets, the price of cotton doubled. Joseph Davis took full advantage of the new opportunities. His name began to appear in newspapers as a prominent attorney in Jefferson County legal affairs. By 1815 he owned two slaves, and the next year he bought three more to begin cultivation of

500 acres he had acquired on Coles Creek. In 1817 he added 450 more acres to this plantation. Landownership was the surest avenue to the privileged class, and Davis had begun the accumulation that would eventually win him that coveted status.

By 1816 he was also principal owner of a mercantile firm called Joseph E. Davis & Co., although he left its day-to-day operation to his partners, Michael and Patrick Tiernan. This venture was evidently not very prosperous because they failed to pay for merchandise ordered from a Baltimore kinsman of the Tiernans. From his youthful apprenticeship to a Kentucky merchant Davis had acquired a distaste for this business, and when the Greenville store failed to produce a quick profit he promptly abandoned it.[9]

In the short space of four years Joseph Davis had become a respected citizen of Jefferson County. His legal duties brought him into contact with prominent men whose friendship he cultivated. Among these leaders was Cowles Mead, a Georgian, who had been named secretary of Mississippi Territory by President Jefferson in 1806. The next year, as acting governor, Mead achieved brief fame when he arrested Aaron Burr and his suspected co-conspirators. Subsequently, Mead, joined by George Poindexter, headed a faction that opposed Governor Robert Williams. Under the more harmonious administration of Governor Holmes, Mead continued to be a leader in territorial politics and became deeply involved in the movement to secure statehood. In October 1816, when he journeyed to a meeting on this subject at John Ford's place on the Pearl River, he took as the other representative from Jefferson County his young friend Joseph Davis.

For years, political leaders had disputed whether the territory should be admitted to the Union as one state or be divided into two. Before the war of 1812 those in the Natchez area favored an undivided state. By 1816, however, the Tombigbee district to the east had more than doubled in area as a result of new Indian cessions, and its population was increasing rapidly. Fearing loss of control, many Natchez leaders now sought statehood for the western half of the territory only, while those from the eastern section reversed their former stand and opted for an undivided state. The meeting at John Ford's, called the Pearl River Convention, was attended by representatives elected at meetings in fifteen of the twenty counties of the territory. Three of the missing five counties bordered the Mississippi River, and one of these was the populous Adams, whose county seat was Natchez. Clearly the meeting was dominated by the eastern "indivisibles."

Cowles Mead was chosen to preside at the sessions, which lasted for three days. Joseph Davis played an active role, being named chairman of the committee that drafted "a memorial to the Congress of the United States praying that the Mississippi Territory might be admitted into the Union as a free, sovereign and independent state, with her present limits." The memorial was deemed necessary to counteract the flood of petitions sent to Congress by "a small minority of our fellow-citizens" requesting division of the territory. Among the arguments for maintaining existing boundaries cited by Davis and his committee was the scarcity of population, which in the undivided territory barely reached the sixty thousand required for statehood by the Northwest Ordinance of 1787. Furthermore, the Indians controlled much of the territory and, perhaps reflecting his repeated problems with the indigenous population from earliest childhood to recent military service, Davis argued that they "are so national in their feelings and so tenacious of their lands, that from all probability a century will escape before their title becomes extinct." The memorial described the advantages to the Union offered by an undivided state, including increased military strength on a strategic frontier.[10]

Although four counties opposed this and all other acts of the meeting because they wanted the territory to be divided, the memorial was approved by the other eleven delegates. A mo-tion by Davis asked the territorial legislature to send a similar memorial to Congress, and the absent counties were notified of the convention's actions. Finally, the delegates chose Judge Harry Toulmin to take the memorial to Washington, D.C., and work for its favorable reception. To show their seriousness of purpose the delegates who voted in favor of these actions then each contributed the generous sum of fifty dollars to defray Toulmin's expenses.[11]

William Lattimore, the official delegate to the U.S. Congress from Mississippi Territory, favored the admission of only the western half as a state and was able to counter Toulmin's lobbying efforts. In this he had the aid of southern senators who were eager to add new states from their section. Although some congressmen feared a loss of control to a rapidly growing West, on March 1, 1817, President James Madison signed an act allowing the admission of the western section as the state of Mississippi. The eastern portion was reorganized as the Alabama Territory. In June, according to the terms of this enabling act, eligible voters in the western region chose delegates to a constitutional convention to meet in the territorial capital the following month. Joseph Davis was one of those chosen to represent Jefferson County.

The little town of Washington must have had difficulty accommodating the forty-seven delegates who assembled at the Methodist church on July 7, 1817, to draw up a constitution for the proposed state of Mississippi. Since he had to come some seventeen miles from Greenville, nearly a day's journey on horseback, Davis was undoubtedly one of those who sought shelter in the town's three small hotels, where men were crowded three or four to a bed. When time permitted, the delegates found refreshment and refuge from the summer heat at the spring and baths east of town. There fashionable ladies and gentlemen from Natchez and the surrounding country gathered in the shade to sip the cool water as one traveler noted, "either pure or mixed to their taste . . . [with] wine, liquors, and spirits." Here for three-eighths of a dollar a patron could indulge in a much needed "hot and cold bath."[12]

Just beyond the baths stood Fort Dearborn, where a contingent of United States troops enlivened the scene with frequent parades and reviews. Society, which a contemporary described as "highly cultivated and refined," included politicians and lawyers drawn there by the territorial capital as well as the budding intellectual community at nearby Jefferson College. In the evening, delegates to the convention enjoyed the hospitality of that "gay and fashionable place . . . famous for its wine parties and dinners, usually enlivened by one or two duels directly afterward."[13]

Despite the distractions, the delegates concentrated most of their attention on the business of creating a constitution. The fourteen counties were unevenly represented at the convention because delegates were allotted according to population. As a result, the five counties on the Mississippi sent twenty-four men while the six hill counties had only twelve delegates, scarcely more than the three intervening counties. From the first it was clear that the wealthy slaveholding west was in control. As usual, the voters had chosen not only the wealthiest but also the best educated and most experienced men. The forty-seven delegates included seventeen lawyers, fourteen planters, three farmers, two doctors, two merchants, and a surveyor. Many of them had held political office in the territory, and more were to become government leaders in the new state.

Although Governor Holmes was named president of the convention, George Poindexter of Wilkinson County dominated the proceedings. Poindexter was a cantankerous attorney from Virginia, who had held many territorial offices and had frequently been involved in controversy. He was respected for his abilities but had few personal friends. At the opening of the convention, he and his colleague Cowles Mead from Jefferson

County led their delegations in opposing the formation of a state as then constituted. These die-hard "indivisibles" knew that statehood was imminent but hoped to increase the boundaries of the new state. Joseph Davis remained a loyal member of this faction through numerous unsuccessful votes, partly out of respect for his former mentor Joseph Johnson, who was one of the Wilkinson delegates.

With this threat temporarily overcome, a committee of twenty-one members was appointed to draft a constitution and, after a recess of one week, report it to the convention. Its membership distribution allowed only two delegates from Jefferson County and, unfortunately for Joseph Davis, the older and more influential Cowles Mead and Cato West were chosen. Instead, Davis was named to Poindexter's committee to prepare a memorial to the federal government requesting an extension of the state's boundaries.

When the reconvened members considered the draft constitution, Davis continued to vote with Cowles Mead and the rest of the Jefferson-Wilkinson group on many issues, although he did not hesitate to break with them when he disagreed with their stand. He favored such conservative measures as limiting the franchise to taxpayers and empowering the governor to appoint most state officials. When Poindexter's suggestion for balloting by voice vote was defeated, Davis sought unsuccessfully to accomplish the same thing by requiring each voter to write his name on the back of his ballot. The junior delegate from Jefferson also joined his colleagues in opposing the outlawing of duels, while favoring mandatory service in the militia and, when his proposed compromise failed, naming Natchez as the new state capital. Davis parted company with both Poindexter and Mead by voting to prevent judges from sitting on cases involving relatives or their own interests.

Davis displayed his most independent and liberal behavior in dealing with the sensitive question of slavery. Here, in daring defiance of his fellow planters, he joined only four others in seeking to limit modestly the unbridled powers of a master over a slave. Their proposal would punish masters who were cruel to their slaves by giving the proceeds of the sale of such bondsmen to the poor rather than to their owners. This unpopular violation of the sacred rights of property represented a contradiction of Davis's self-interest as an ambitious and upwardly mobile lawyer-planter striving to accumulate land and slaves. His stance can only be explained as evidence of his lifelong concern for the welfare of slaves and his ambivalence about the morality of the institution. Having grown up with one or two blacks who shared the hardships of frontier life with his family, Davis never lost the ability to see them as humans with the same feelings as whites. Even as early as 1817, this sensitivity set him apart.

After six weeks of hard work and frequent compromise in the midsummer heat, the convention finally agreed on a constitution. On August 15, all the delegates affixed their signatures to it except John Shaw, who had died during the proceedings, and Cato West, who, one historian claims, "never found anything with which he could agree." The document was not unique; large sections of it were taken from the constitutions of Kentucky, Tennessee, and Louisiana. It was more conservative than most western charters for it required property and religious qualifications of officeholders, and only the governor and lieutenant governor were popularly elected. Nevertheless, its framers and most of their constituents seemed pleased with the document, although it was never submitted to popular vote. On December 10, when President Monroe signed the resolution of admission, Joseph Davis had two events to celebrate—his thirty-third birthday and the entrance of Mississippi into the Union.[14]

Davis returned to Greenville from the constitutional convention to find his reputation enhanced and his contacts with men of distinction broadened. As his law practice grew, he began investing surplus income in land farther away. In early 1818 he bought a tract on the Pearl River in Marion County. In May he joined with a friend, Littleton Henderson, to purchase more than 7,000 acres of rich bottomland on a bend of the Mississippi River. The land was located in Warren County a few miles below the Walnut Hills, later the town of Vicksburg. Davis thought the latter site so promising that he soon acquired an additional 548 acres from the government in his own name and bought out Henderson. Over the next few years he purchased the small farms scattered through and adjoining this land on Palmyra Bend, which would become Davis Bend.[15]

His position as a prominent man of property widened Joseph Davis's social contacts. In 1819 he was admitted to membership in the Masonic Lodge of Mississippi, meeting at Natchez, whose members included some of the leading lawyers and planters of the state. At the urging of his associates, he agreed to another foray into the political arena, and in the fall of 1819 he was elected to the state House of Representatives from Jefferson County.

In January 1820 the legislature of the young state met in what one observer described as "a kind of superior hay-loft" in a house in Natchez. Davis, arriving from Greenville two days late, was appointed to several committees, including one to deal with the governor's recommendations for improving the judiciary and another to revise the criminal law of the state. He introduced and won approval of "an Act to take the Census of the State of Mississippi" but failed to get enacted a bill to establish public schools or one to emancipate a slave woman belonging to his physician, Benjamin Bullen. Perhaps most important for his future interests, Davis was appointed to a committee to consider a levee project for Warren County and one to investigate the advisability of banning the importation of slaves into the state. Neither committee achieved results that session.[16]

In early February Richard C. Langdon, editor of the *Mississippi Republican* and newly named public printer, was called before the House to answer contempt charges for publishing critical pieces "calculated to disturb the coolness and deliberation of that body." In spite of a spirited defense by Joseph E. Davis, Langdon was dismissed from office by a vote of seventeen to ten. This and other partisan acts he observed may have disillusioned Davis, for by the time the session ended on February 10 this novice solon had decided not to stand for reelection.[17]

If the actions of the legislature proved disappointing to Davis, his stay in Natchez certainly did not. Compared with the declining village of Greenville, Natchez seemed a model of metropolitan charm. It was the commercial as well as the political center for the region, unrivaled between New Orleans and St. Louis. Every day steamboats and flatboats crowded the landing in the notorious "Under-the-Hill" section. Here the single street contained ramshackle boardinghouses for riverboatmen, a few shops, bawdy houses, and a tavern or two. Old flatboats served as temporary docks and warehouses through which passed an amazing variety of merchandise and farm products. Much of it moved up the steep causeway to the town proper on the bluff above, where attractive brick and frame buildings lined tree-shaded streets neatly laid out at right angles in the familiar grid pattern.

This pleasant site had been occupied for a long time, first by the Natchez Indians, then successively by the French, the British, and the Spanish, all of whom had left their mark. Even after a quarter-century of American control, visitors often remarked on the cosmopolitan mix of people who crowded the open marketplace. In 1820 a disproportionate share of the three thousand inhabitants were affluent planters, lawyers, and merchants, who were able to maintain and enhance the social and cultural milieu inherited from earlier occupants.

In addition to a city hall, jail, firehouse, markethouse, and new two-story hospital, the town boasted a theater housed in the former hospital. Although social life tended to center in the fine homes of the well-to-do, informal gatherings were held at the coffee house, the hotel, or the reading room. Though its political dominance would decline as newer parts of the state united against it, Natchez in 1820 was the undisputed metropolis of Mississippi.[18]

Natchez society was dominated by a group of Adams County families who had accumulated considerable wealth from business ventures, especially the sale of cotton produced on their fertile plantations manned by slave labor. They were connected by a confusing network of intermarriage, business partnerships, and political alliances and included among their number the leading lawyers of the state. These men established their rank in the aristocracy by building impressive mansions in or near the town, where they dispensed elaborate hospitality at every opportunity. One visitor described the delightful days of such a visit, starting with mint juleps sent to his room before a sumptuous breakfast on the veranda. Then, he said, "we hunt, ride, fish, pay morning visits, play chess, read or lounge" until dinner at two o'clock, when a great variety of rich and "delicately cooked" foods were consumed in leisurely fashion. Afterward the guests dispersed for a siesta, reassembling at sunset at the tea table set under the oaks. The visitor concluded, "Then, until bed-time, we stroll, sing, play whist or croquet. It is an indolent, yet charming life." Although most of the "nabobs" and their wives were busier than this description indicates, they enjoyed a relatively luxurious life-style for a rural community.[19]

After sampling the pleasures of Natchez society for a month, Joseph Davis determined on a course that he had been considering for some time—he would move his practice to that exciting city. He put his Jefferson County property up for sale, and in April the *Mississippi State Gazette* announced that "Thos. B. Reed and Jos. E. Davis, attornies and counsellors at law, have entered into partnership in their profession and will practice in the counties of Claiborne, Jefferson, Adams, Franklin, and Wilkinson." The notice directed clients to Reed's office "opposite the house in which the Legislature held its late Session" and promised that one of the partners would always be found there. Furthermore, Reed said that while he was absent "on the circuit," Davis would take care of his clients.[20]

Davis was indeed advancing his prestige as well as his fortunes by entering this partnership. Thomas B. Reed was a leading member of the Mississippi bar, soon to be named attorney general. He continued in this office for the duration of their partnership and was then elected to the U.S. Senate. He died in office at the age of forty-two. A Kentuckian a few years younger than Davis, Reed had arrived in Natchez a decade earlier and quickly established a reputation as a talented lawyer. By the early 1820s he had joined the ranks of the nabobs, boasting a modest fortune, a mansion staffed by slaves, and considerable cotton land. His success was achieved despite a cold personality that made him appear haughty and condescending toward others. Nevertheless, he was an astute lawyer, and positions in his law office were eagerly sought by young men such as Spence M. Grayson, who had just arrived from Virginia to accept one. Having made his reputation in Greenville and at the constitutional convention, Joseph Davis started his Natchez career in a position that commanded respect.[21]

Natchez, where the most eminent lawyers gathered for sessions of the legislature as well as meetings of the circuit and supreme courts, was the focal point for the legal profession of Mississippi. A year after Davis moved his legal practice there, a few of the more influential of these jurists established the first formally incorporated state bar association in the United States. The leader of this organization was Edward Turner, a Virginia-born, Kentucky-trained lawyer who had been a member of the state constitutional convention. He had also served two terms as speaker of the Mississippi House of Representatives, including the 1820 session of which Davis was a member. Turner, a

wealthy planter in Adams County, also owned a large plantation in Warren County adjacent to the land Davis had recently
bought, so it is not surprising that Davis was invited to join the
new bar association. At its first election Edward Turner was
elected president, and his son-in-law William B. Griffith became
secretary. In addition, four men were named to the powerful
standing committee. Among these were Thomas B. Reed and
Joseph E. Davis, both of whom served throughout the four-year
life of the association. Membership was by invitation only, and
applicants deemed unworthy were refused entry. The purpose of
the organization, according to Turner, was to protect standards
of the profession; in that rapidly growing new state self-styled
lawyers flocked in with the immigrants and set up practice despite their lack of credentials. The bar association struggled
with the question of setting stricter requirements for licensing
but could agree only on asking the attorney general and the two
other "distinguished attorneys" of the examining committee to
be diligent in determining the competence and morality of applicants for a license.

The rules and regulations of the bar association included a
detailed list of the lowest fees that a member was allowed to
charge for professional services. They ranged from five dollars
for "verbal advice and opinion" or ten if it was written, to a
fifty-dollar original retainer in a supreme court case and one
hundred for "mixed and real actions." The fixed fee system and
restrictive policy toward new members were intended to protect
these attorneys' profitable and exclusive positions in the profession. Since at its maximum the association included no more
than 40 percent of the state's lawyers, mere membership undoubtedly added to their prestige and perhaps to their fees.
In 1824, after his appointment to the supreme court bench,
Edward Turner resigned from the bar association and Joseph
Davis was chosen to be the new president. He had now reached
the pinnacle of the Mississippi bar.[22]

Davis's eminence in the highly competitive legal profession was based upon proven ability. One observer noted that his "intellectual vigor . . . inquisitiveness of mind . . .[and] practicality of disposition" led him to view cases "in the light of reason and stern reality." With his excellent memory for detail that contributed to the depth of his legal knowledge, Davis was able to see the broad picture and then focus on the crucial point with logical precision. Furthermore, a contemporary reported that "to his powers of analysis and synthesis were superadded superior oratorical accomplishments"—an important skill in a society that admired flowery rhetoric. Davis was a small, well-dressed, handsome man whose quietly compelling manner made him "a powerful advocate." No wonder a competitor vowed he would rather have anyone but Joe Davis oppose him in the courtroom.[23]

As the profits from his legal practice accumulated, Davis began investing in real estate in the rapidly expanding, capital-hungry city of Natchez, buying lots at public auction or financing mortgages for friends and business associates. Among his purchases were a lot and building near the landing next to "the old Kentucky tavern" in Natchez-Under-the-Hill; unfortunately, official deeds do not record whether it was used as a boarding-house or a bordello. In 1822 Davis bought a forty-foot lot on Main Street, including a nice house which probably became his principal residence. By 1823 he owned city property worth $8,000 in addition to his plantation holdings and still had a bank balance of nearly $5,000.

This prosperous attorney was now in a position to enjoy the social and cultural life of Natchez to the fullest. He was advancing through the ranks of the Masonic Lodge, becoming grand junior warden in 1822 and grand senior warden the next year. When the Masons staged a lottery to earn money for "a Grand Masonic hall," Davis was one of the nine managers, along with his next-door neighbor Henry Postelthwaite and fellow bar member Edward Turner.

Although there is no indication that Davis felt any strong doctrinal preference for the Episcopal faith, in 1822, when some wealthy friends were planning a wedding and noted the lack of a suitable minister and church for the affair, he joined them in founding Trinity Episcopal Church. Within a year they had called a minister and erected a church for which Davis served as a vestryman along with Edward Turner, Stephen Duncan, William Minor, and others of the Natchez elite.

Joseph Davis enjoyed many activities less solemn than meetings of the church or the Masons. He loved purebred horses and spent some time and money at the racetrack on the edge of town. He also enjoyed the theatrical performances that since 1806 had made Natchez a haven of culture in the wilderness. Both amateur members of the Natchez Theatrical Association and professional road companies presented plays. The traveling players who made their way up and down the river were often as shabby in costume and lacking in talent as local thespians, but their audiences were generally uncritical and their performances added a cosmopolitan aura to the community.

Davis especially enjoyed studying philosophical subjects, and he joined Benjamin L. C. Wailes in forming the Adams Athenaeum. At monthly meetings members presented papers on a variety of topics for criticism and discussion. Davis also heartily endorsed the Athenaeum's objective of establishing a library containing books and "most of the public journals of merit in the Union."[24]

Occasionally some important national or international figure traveling along the Mississippi stopped at Natchez to receive a gala welcome from the townspeople. In the spring of 1825 the French hero of the American Revolution, the Marquis de Lafayette, made a triumphal tour of the nation he had helped to free some fifty years earlier. On the way from New Orleans to St. Louis his entourage of distinguished military and political leaders stopped for about twelve hours for the most elaborate celebration Natchez could provide. General Lafayette was greeted by a military salute and a grand parade made up of the uniformed militia, members of the state legislature, the courts, and the county government, "Gentlemen of the Bar," as well as citizens on foot and on horseback. They escorted him from the landing up the bluff to the town proper. The parade proceeded down Main Street to the common for speeches before winding through the town to Purnell's Hotel. There, after a brief rest, the general was given an elaborate banquet at which the local dignitaries offered toasts to him, to France, to the United States, and to their mutual friendship. After the tables were cleared away, there was a gala ball and members of the general's party mingled with the Natchez elite in merrymaking until one o'clock in the morning, when another procession accompanied the guests back to their steamboat. Local newspapers congratulated the citizens on a successful celebration: "The weather was very fine, the utmost harmony prevailed, [and] not an accident happened to mar the pleasure of the day and evening."[25]

Lafayette's visit may have been especially interesting for Joseph Davis, not only because he was introduced to the renowned Frenchman but also because of the opportunity to meet another stimulating visitor. Frances Wright, a charming and well-educated young British woman of strong views, was traveling in the general's party. During an earlier visit to North America, this student of philosophy and protégé of great men had written a book favorably contrasting the freedoms and innovations of the new nation with tradition-bound European society. Naturally, this won her acclaim in the United States. During this second visit, however, Wright saw more to criticize. She was especially appalled by black slavery as practiced in America and sought possible remedies for this serious flaw in an otherwise admirable society.

On her way across the country to meet Lafayette in New Orleans, she had detoured to visit Harmonie, a prosperous village in western Indiana built by the industrious and pious Rappites. Robert Owen, the renowned Scottish industrialist, had just bought the town as the site for his proposed new ideal community. Owen's model factory town at New Lanark, Scotland, had won international approval for its pleasant accommodations and humane treatment of workers, and now in this promising new setting he proposed to demonstrate more fully his theory of the efficacy of cooperation for mutual advantage. Frances Wright was intrigued with the bold new venture, which embodied many of the principles that she had come to accept. Gradually she evolved a scheme that would apply Owen's methods to slavery, which she saw as America's greatest problem. Deciding that she herself would take the first steps to eradicate that evil, she proposed to establish a model plantation in the South where the slaves she would purchase could work to earn their own emancipation while being trained to provide for themselves as freedmen. Wright was eager to discuss this scheme with the men who knew the most about running a slave plantation—successful planters—so at this stop on the trip upriver she sought out the Natchez nabobs.

Davis was undoubtedly fascinated by this articulate, well-informed, and worldly woman. He had been pondering the very questions she raised concerning the viability and desirability of slavery and its possible alternatives. The previous year he had established his brother Isaac and family on the five-thousand-acre plantation in Warren County, where, with the labor of more than fifty slaves, he hoped to create a remunerative cotton enterprise. Many Mississippi planters, like their counterparts throughout the South, privately questioned the morality or practicality of the "peculiar institution." Like Thomas Jefferson a generation earlier, they sought answers to the twin problems of where to find an alternative source of labor for their rapidly expanding agricultural operations and what to do with the former slaves if they were freed. By the 1820s the cotton gin and vast acres of newly opened fertile land had made cotton culture a most profitable activity, but reflective southerners experienced the same ethical qualms that would soon bring emancipation to the British colonies in the Caribbean and the abolitionist movement to the northern United States. A decade later emancipation would become a forbidden topic among the group of southerners who in 1825 listened with interest to Wright's utopian scheme.[26]

This was a year of great restlessness for Joseph Davis; he had turned forty the previous December, and perhaps he was experiencing a midlife crisis, although such terms of introspection were unknown in that pre-Freudian era. As the oldest and certainly the most prosperous member of his large family, Davis felt an increasing weight of responsibility. His father had unwisely cosigned some notes that were overdue, and Joseph came to his rescue, buying his farm near Woodville in 1822. Two years later, when the elder Davis had a disagreement with Samuel, his third son and partner in farming, the old man took his slaves up the river from Woodville to Joseph's plantation at Davis Bend, where Isaac was the manager. The feud and the rigors of the river journey proved too much for him, and Samuel Davis the elder sickened and died there on July 4, 1824. Now Joseph was, indeed, the head of the large family, with full responsibility for his mother and sixteen-year-old brother, Jefferson. Through his political contacts in Natchez, Joseph secured an appointment to the U.S. Military Academy at West Point for the reluctant lad, who arrived there in September 1824. Concerned about the boy who seemed to him more like a son than a brother, Joseph decided to make the long trek to upstate New York the next summer to visit him.[27]

Although Davis could have taken a leave of absence from his law practice, he decided instead to dissolve his partnership with Thomas B. Reed. After five years as the junior partner, perhaps Davis wanted the autonomy and financial benefits of practicing alone. By now, having been elected president of the bar association the previous December, he was certainly well established as one of the outstanding lawyers in Natchez and would have no trouble attracting as many clients as he chose to serve.[28]

Davis recruited some compatible companions to join him on the New York trip. When William B. Howell, son of the governor of New Jersey, came to Mississippi in 1815, Davis befriended the tall, amiable former army officer and sponsored him in local society. Howell was enchanted by the beautiful Margaret Kempe, daughter of wealthy landowner James Kempe, who had commanded the dragoon company in which Davis served briefly in 1813. By 1823 Margaret had accepted Howell's proposal of marriage, and Davis served as groomsman at their wedding at Trinity Episcopal church. The next year the young couple named their first child Joseph Davis Howell in honor of their good friend. When the infant proved unhealthy, Davis suggested that they remove him from Natchez in the summer "sickly season" by sharing the trip to New York. Considering the rigors of nineteenth-century travel, this seems a questionable idea, but the Howells readily agreed.[29]

Setting out from Natchez in early June, the travelers could take a steamboat up the Mississippi and Ohio rivers to Pittsburgh. Travel by boat was not only faster but also much smoother and more comfortable than journeying overland. The water level on the Ohio was low at that time, and, like a party that immediately preceded them, when their boat could no longer navigate the river they had to make part of the trip from Louisville by stagecoach or wagon. This tedious mode of travel was their only option when they turned north from Pittsburgh across Pennsylvania to Lake Erie. The road was so poor that they averaged less than three miles an hour. One can imagine their fatigue after twelve hours of jouncing on a bench in a crowded coach, whose thin leather side curtains did not keep out the cold wind and rain on bad days and when rolled up to admit the breeze on hot days covered the passengers with dust from the road. They could look forward to little relief at night when a local inn would provide only a crude meal and a soiled bed to be shared with other wayfarers. Enduring such a venture with a sickly baby required great patience.

On June 24, 1825, the Davis party found some diversion on the slow journey across western Pennsylvania. When their stage stopped in Meadville, they were joined by the famous Robert Owen and his companions. This was a great thrill for Joseph Davis, who had not only heard Fanny Wright sing Owen's praises but had read his book *A New View of Society,* as well as glowing accounts of his recent appearances in eastern cities. At well-publicized receptions the previous winter in New York, Philadelphia, and Washington, Owen had been entertained by such men as President James Monroe and President-elect John Quincy Adams; at Speaker of the House Henry Clay's invitation he had given two addresses at the Capitol, each attended by members of the cabinet, the Supreme Court, and the Congress. With letters of introduction from President Monroe, he had called on former presidents Jefferson and Madison in the course of his triumphal tour to Indiana. Now this social reformer, who was on his way back to Britain to win more support and recruits for his New Harmony venture, was eager to expound his theories about the advantages of cooperation for human productivity and happiness. For nine long hours Joseph Davis had an opportunity to hear and argue these questions, and he was profoundly impressed with Owen's ideas.[30]

That night, when their stage reached Erie on the lake, they discovered that the steamboat to Buffalo was not expected for two days so Owen and his party decided to make the trip overland. Davis and the Howells evidently chose to wait in the comparative comfort of the inn; in fact, those who braved the rough two-day stage journey arrived in Buffalo only a few hours before the boat.

Continuing their leisurely journey, the Davis-Howell party reached Lockport, New York, where they were among the earliest users of a remarkable man-made wonder—the new Erie Canal. This modern highway from Buffalo to Albany was begun in 1817 but not formally opened until October 1825, although by midsummer travelers were using all but the last stretch. Designed mainly for freight transport, the canal cut the cost per mile from nearly twenty cents to less than one cent per ton and launched the nation on the Canal Age. It gave the travelers from Mississippi a smooth journey of four or five days at three or four miles an hour in the crowded but comfortable canal boat to Albany, where they boarded a Hudson River boat to West Point. There young Jefferson Davis greeted them enthusiastically, and for the next week Joseph enjoyed attending to his family duties. But sometimes amid the merriment, and frequently on the long trip home with many stops at springs and spas, Davis had time to meditate on the communal solution to social problems advocated by Robert Owen and its possible application to the problem of slavery as suggested by Fanny Wright.[31]

During the next two years, as Davis continued his Natchez law practice, he gradually made the decision to give up his life as a member of the elite there and retire as resident planter on his rich riverside plantation in Warren County. A number of factors combined to make this move seem desirable. By the late 1820s Natchez was no longer the unrivaled political and economic center of Mississippi that it had been when he migrated to the territory a decade and a half before. The influence of other counties had forced the removal of the state capital in 1821. Five years later, the supreme court, the last state government body in Natchez, moved to Jackson, and the Natchez representation in the lower house of the state legislature was cut in half. In 1827 Thomas Reed, Davis's former law partner, was defeated for the U.S. Senate by a man described by one historian as "a popular champion of the piney-woods folk." This populist trend continued the next year when a revision of the judicial districts ended the dominant influence of Natchez attorneys in the circuit courts of the interior counties. Davis's professional position as a leader of the Natchez bar was no longer as exciting as it had seemed when he first moved to Natchez.[32]

Joseph Davis came to believe that his planting enterprise required his full attention if it were to achieve the prosperity he desired. His brother Isaac, as manager of the Warren County operation, had been making progress with the difficult task of clearing and cultivating land in that lush area along the Mississippi. He was making a name for himself, too, having been appointed justice of the peace in Warren County in 1825. But he and Joseph did not always agree about the best methods of managing the land or the growing force of slaves. As one family member noted years later, Isaac "was too much like his brother Joe (too masterful) for them to get on well together in business." Their partnership ended dramatically in 1827, when a tornado struck the plantation, destroying the house, breaking Isaac's leg, and killing his infant son. The grieving parents determined to leave the plantation that would henceforth be called Hurricane. Joseph was faced with the immediate problem of managing his most promising economic venture.[33]

Many other gentlemen planters in the South faced and solved such problems without giving up their legal careers and isolating themselves on their lands. Although the desire to own a prosperous cotton plantation was almost universal in that era and planting was the basis of most of the fortunes that were made, the leaders of Natchez society usually resided in the city and employed overseers to manage their holdings. Had Joseph Davis followed the normal pattern for men in his position, he might well have turned for new challenges to a political career. Having served in the original constitutional convention and then been elected to the state legislature even before moving to Natchez, he could have used his prominent position and wide contacts for further political advancement. In fact, despite a keen interest in politics, except for an abortive attempt to win a place at the next constitutional convention in 1832, he never again stood for elective office nor accepted a political appointment.

To demonstrate the extent of Davis's deviation from the norm, it is instructive to compare his accomplishments with those of another Natchez nabob who went on to become a leading figure in Mississippi politics. John A. Quitman arrived in Natchez almost two years after Davis with far fewer credentials. He was twenty-two years old instead of thirty-six. He had practiced law only briefly in Ohio, not for nine years in an adjoining county, and of course had never held elective office in Mississippi. Furthermore, Quitman had total assets of only $15 while Davis arrived with $10,000 in the bank. Joseph Davis was one of three examiners for the high court of errors and appeals who admitted Quitman to the bar in 1822 just a month after his arrival. The new lawyer immediately started working for William B. Griffith, a prominent attorney, who made him a partner the next year. Quitman, who had been a member of the Masons in Ohio, joined the Natchez lodge in 1822 and rose even more rapidly than Davis, achieving the state's highest office, grand master, in 1826. Davis had advanced in the organization from 1819 to 1823 after which he became less active.

Although he was not one of the founders as Davis had been, Quitman became an active member of Trinity Episcopal Church. He was admitted to the Mississippi State Bar Association in 1823 and served on its ruling standing committee; the society dissolved before he could serve as president. Unhampered by Davis's prejudice against military service, Quitman organized a militia troop, the popular Natchez Fencibles, and served as its captain through many public drills and parades.

Up to this point the two men seem to have had comparable success; both had the public recognition and prominent friends to launch them on political careers—except for one factor. Two years after his arrival in town, Quitman married Eliza Turner, the sixteen-year-old daughter of one of the state's wealthiest planters, and by 1826 he had bought Monmouth, an impressive estate with a majestic mansion on the outskirts of Natchez. At age twenty-five John Quitman had assembled all the attributes necessary for a career of political prominence.[34]

In contrast, as he entered his forties, Joseph Davis had apparently never married. There is no record of his marriage in the archives of Mississippi, Kentucky, or Tennessee. Nor is there in all the land transactions recorded during his prosperous years—more than a dozen instruments in which he is grantor or grantee between May 1821 and August 1827—any mention of a spouse. Had he been married, anyone buying property from him would have required a wife's signature on the deed. Nor in family tradition is there any mention of a wife before 1827. This lack of a spouse did not mean that Davis was uninterested in feminine company; on the contrary, both contemporary accounts and later traditions note his admiration for charming members of the opposite sex. His Kentucky liaison with Rachel Shelby, which apparently resulted in the birth of a boy, William Davis, has already been noted. His reputation as a ladies' man has persisted to this day.

Perhaps he could have overcome the social handicap of his lack of a hostess in Natchez, but as a further indication of his unorthodoxy, Joseph Davis acknowledged and provided for three daughters whose mother or mothers he had evidently never married. Florida Ann Davis, who accompanied him on the trip to West Point in 1825, had been born in 1811, either in Mississippi or Tennessee (census returns give conflicting reports) while Joseph was migrating from Kentucky to the Mississippi Territory. Like her sisters, she did not live with her father but was accepted by him and the family, as is evidenced by her later claim to have been a schoolmate of her Uncle Jefferson, perhaps in Greenville or Washington, and by her correspondence with him in early 1825. Next in age was Mary Lucinda Davis, born in Mississippi in 1816, while her father was building his law practice and his fortune in Greenville. Finally, there was Caroline, born in 1823, when Joseph Davis had achieved prosperity and prominence in Natchez. To have children outside of marriage was not unusual for that or any era, but to acknowledge them publicly was unacceptable even in a frontier community. Perhaps Davis's concern about the status of his daughters in the mid-1820s indicates the evolution of Natchez to a more rigid, straitlaced society. He may have begun to feel that the children made his advancement along traditional lines impossible. Or he may merely have wanted to live with his daughters in a stable family situation where they would be free from social slights.

In any case, on October 5, 1827, Joseph E. Davis, age forty-three, married Eliza Van Benthuysen, age sixteen, at Trinity Episcopal Church in Natchez. The bride was one of a large family. Her widowed mother, Mary, who had operated a "Boot and Shoe Store" on Main Street in Natchez more than a decade earlier, was now mistress of a boardinghouse in New Orleans. Eliza was no beauty according to family portraits, but her later correspondence shows her to have been a very intelligent, articulate woman.[35] Whatever his reasons for deciding to marry this late in his life and for choosing a spouse a few months younger than his eldest daughter, never throughout their long marriage did Joseph Davis falter in his consideration for her. Theirs seems to have been a truly loving relationship. In the fall of 1827 Joseph Davis abandoned his career in Natchez and took his bride and three daughters up the river to begin their new life at Hurricane Plantation in Warren County.

THREE

Antebellum Planter Patriarch

HURRICANE PLANTATION, where Joseph Davis was to spend the next thirty-five years, occupied more than five thousand acres of rich bottomland on a bend of the Mississippi River. Davis had bought most of the land on this peninsula some fifteen miles below Vicksburg, which came to be known as Davis Bend. He sold portions to people he thought would make good neighbors but reserved for himself the southwestern section with some five miles of riverfront.

The land, covered with dense brush, was punctuated by small lakes and sloughs, where white and blue cranes balanced on one leg among large yellow water lilies. In the fall great flocks of wild geese and ducks crowded these waters. Here too were found giant alligators capable of swallowing small animals, even calves that strayed too near the bank. The higher ground held luxurious stands of hardwood, where deer and wildcats made their home. The rank vegetation and swarms of insects gave the impression of an almost tropical lushness.[1]

Clearing the rich uplands to plant cash crops was an arduous and time-consuming task that challenged the work force. The cane and briers were too thick to be uprooted; instead, the slaves burned the underbrush, then dug small holes in which they planted cottonseed. The first crops were unusually bountiful and helped defray the cost of buying more slaves to clear additional fields.

At first, the modest plantation house built after the destructive storm of 1827 seemed adequate for Davis, his bride, and three daughters, but soon the steady stream of relatives and friends who sojourned there for varying lengths of time led the Davises to plan a larger place. By 1834 their continuing prosperity allowed them to start construction of a proper mansion, comparable to those of their Natchez acquaintances. This major project required a great deal of labor. In addition to the slaves, who cut most of the timber and made all of the bricks on the plantation, Davis employed skilled craftsmen and supervisors. At one point Eliza reported, "We have quite a Colony here—seven Carpenters[,] two brick layers & one *Physician,*" in addition to a visiting family of five. She found it necessary to house them in the hospital normally reserved for the slaves.[2]

This protracted inconvenience was more than justified by the final results. A decade later, numerous guests described the fine accommodations they enjoyed at Hurricane. One called it "an ideal home of hospitality, culture, and luxury." Visitors arrived either from the landing, the usual approach because the river was the main artery of travel, or from the Warrenton road via a broad circular drive bounded by rows of live oak. The massive house of stucco-covered brick was three stories tall with broad, two-storied galleries all around. The walls were thick and the windows small, lending a cavelike coolness to the interior that was especially welcome in the long, hot summers. The damp chill of winter was dispelled by large fireplaces in most of the twelve rooms. Downstairs a wide entry hall separated the drawing room and ladies' tearoom on the right from the master bedroom and office. Joseph Davis often retired to the office with gentlemen callers for long discussions of politics, law, the economy, and world affairs.

Each of the two upper floors contained four large bedrooms as well as a bathroom. Installed by plumbers brought down from Cincinnati, these rare conveniences were supplied with water from a huge tank in the attic, which was filled by a slave-powered force pump in the well.

A large wing was connected to the main house at one corner by a walkway from the upstairs porch, which covered the brick path below. This wing contained only two rooms, each forty-three feet long and twenty-five feet wide. The lower one was a red-brick-paved dining room large enough to accommodate a houseful of guests. Above was a music room with high, curved ceiling and portrait-covered walls. Here could be found a piano, guitars, sometimes a harp, as well as music books and sheet music. This was where the young people played, sang, danced, and improvised theatrical performances. Serving much the same function as a modern recreation room, this salon removed younger visitors from sedate adult company and allowed people with diverse interests to enjoy themselves.

Behind this wing stood a two-story brick building that may have been the original house. By the 1840s its lower floor was used for the kitchen, storeroom, and laundry with six bedrooms above for the house servants. Behind this, yet another building housed the overseer's office and storeroom with two bedrooms upstairs.

In the 1840s, as the number of residents increased, Joseph Davis gave up his office in the main house. A short distance from the mansion toward the river he constructed a replica of a Greek temple with columns around all four sides. It contained two large rooms, each with a fireplace at one end and large bay windows and French doors at the other. One of these rooms became the library and, when the mansion was full, served as bachelor quarters. The other room became Davis's new office, a retreat comfortably removed from the hubbub of the house.

The mansion, situated on a low rise about a quarter of a mile back from the river, was surrounded by beautifully landscaped grounds. A parklike meadow stretching up from the river was dotted with handsome trees and shrubs, some of them native, including live oak, pecan, magnolia, and camellia. There were also more exotic plants from Europe and Asia, either gifts of friends and neighbors or ordered from agents in New Orleans.

A broad walk shaded by crepe myrtle trees led from the back gallery to the garden, which covered many acres and was surrounded by a luxuriant hedge of roses, honeysuckle, and jasmine. Here could be seen a wide variety of artistically arranged shrubs. One relative noted, "The whole family was addicted to gardening, and whenever they heard of some new plant, it had to be ordered at once." Davis hired an English gardener to supervise the arrangement and maintenance. The garden was so spectacular that sometimes passing riverboats would stop to give their passengers a better view.[3]

Beyond the flower garden were eight acres of well-tended orchards containing peach, apple, pear, quince, and plum trees. Nearby was a large vegetable garden that provided bountifully for all the residents, black and white. In season the surplus from these sources was sold either to passing steamboats or to markets in Vicksburg or New Orleans.

Intersecting the garden walk, another path led to the stables, where some thirty stalls accommodated Davis's purebred horses. Nearby stood a group of utility buildings housing a blacksmith shop, corncrib, cotton gin, and grist and sawmills. When steam power was introduced in the 1830s, Joseph Davis was among the first Mississippians to adopt it so the gin and mills were driven by a huge steam engine.[4]

Beyond the stable lots and, as time went on, in other parts of the plantation as well were clustered neat rows of slave houses.

Here Joseph Davis demonstrated the enlightened methods of slave management that he had developed from modifications of the ideas of Robert Owen, Frances Wright, and other reformers of an earlier era. In the words of a family member, "[The cabins] were well built, with plastered walls and large fireplaces, two large rooms and two shed rooms behind them." Each had its own henhouse from which the slaves could sell surplus chickens and eggs and a small garden patch for their own use.[5]

Joseph Davis's growing prosperity was reflected in the number of his slaves. He understood full well that development of a successful plantation was directly dependent upon the size of its labor force, so he invested a large proportion of his profits in additional slaves. In the decade of the 1830s, besides building and furnishing the mansion, he acquired some 114 new bondsmen, increasing his total slave force to 226. The economic downturns of 1837 and 1839 seemed to bring little immediate change in his actions, although the attendant drop in the price of cotton probably contributed to his decision to slow his slave purchases between 1838 and 1842. In 1843 cotton that had sold for more than fifteen cents a pound eight years earlier brought less than six cents a pound, but after adding only 5 slaves in the previous five years, Davis bought 15 new laborers that year. For the entire decade of the 1840s, however, the Davis slave community grew by only 16.

The boom years of the next decade brought the master of Hurricane to the zenith of his economic achievement. He was one of those fortunate few planters whose large cotton plantations developed agriculture to the highest levels of efficiency, complexity, and commercialization to be found anywhere in America before the Civil War. Outside the South the shortage of hired labor generally limited the size of farms to the acreage that one family could cultivate. However, in the South a planter could purchase as many slaves as he could afford, thus allowing able managers to accumulate a large labor force to cultivate many acres. Joseph Davis used all his business acumen to built an estate that by 1860 included 345 slaves cultivating more than seventeen hundred acres of improved land.

Davis strove to make Hurricane a model plantation in many ways. He read the leading agricultural journals and corresponded with other planters practicing scientific farming. One contemporary later observed that, although Davis "was not famous for the number of his cotton bales, they were always of the best quality." Although cotton was the major cash crop at Hurricane, Davis also marketed a variety of other produce. For example, in 1850 he raised fifteen thousand bushels of Indian corn while his neighbor Edward Turner produced only ten thousand bushels on a plantation of comparable size. In addition, Davis harvested a thousand bushels of sweet potatoes and one hundred hogs, which along with the $1,000 worth of orchard produce must have made Hurricane nearly self-sufficient. In 1850 Davis was the only planter on the bend to keep a large herd of sheep (two hundred head) and enough cattle to produce five hundred pounds of butter as well as $1,000 worth of beef. Ten years later, just before the outbreak of the war, he was producing more of all of these items while adding buckwheat, peas, and beans to the list. He thoroughly enjoyed the risks and rewards involved in scientific agriculture.[6]

Davis was determined to make his enterprise a model of labor management as well. As one of only nine Mississippians who owned more than three hundred slaves in 1860, Davis was faced with a major administrative task; he chose some very innovative methods of slave management in an effort to transfer some of Robert Owen's principles of cooperation from a factory town to an agricultural slave community. From his experience on the farm and in the store in Kentucky, as well as in his law practice in Mississippi, Davis had learned that people worked best when treated well and given incentives rather than when driven by fear of punishment. He heartily disagreed with the prevailing view among slaveholders that "the most important part of management of slaves is always to keep them under proper subjection. . . . Unconditional submission is the only footing upon which slavery should be placed." Reflecting his own individualistic abhorrence of authoritarianism, Davis maintained, "The less people are governed, the more submissive they will be to control." Implementing this belief, he set up an unusual form of self-government among his work force on the plantation. He established a court, eventually held every Sunday in a small building called the Hall of Justice, where a slave jury heard complaints of slave misconduct and the testimony of the accused in their own defense. No slave was punished except upon conviction by this jury of peers. Sitting as the judge, Davis seldom intervened except to ameliorate the severity of some of the sentences. One contemporary reported, "[Davis] gave it as his experience that the tendency of his plantation juries, like those of other courts, was to find a verdict not from the evidence adduced, but from their opinion of the character of the accused, a disposition which it became necessary for him to check by the most careful charges and an un-judgelike defence of the criminal."[7]

Davis insisted that the overseers, too, must bring their complaints before the court, and they could not punish a slave without its permission. This diminution of their power caused many of these men to claim that they could not maintain discipline, but Davis seldom compromised his system at their behest. Although the daily management of the work force was under their direction, the overseers knew that Joseph Davis was likely to turn up at any moment with a sympathetic ear for his bondsmen. As a result, Hurricane must have been considered an undesirable place of employment for white overseers.

In addition to self-government, Davis provided more direct incentives for his laborers. Convinced that every human being should be allowed to develop his full potential, the master encouraged his slaves to acquire skills in areas that interested them. He provided opportunities for training in current trades and crafts. Moreover, skilled workers were allowed to enjoy the benefits of their more valuable labor; Davis ruled that all slaves might keep anything they earned beyond the value of their labor as field hands.

Only a few slaves became skilled craftsmen, but most of them profited from other incentives Davis provided. With unlimited supplies of feed available, most raised chickens because they could sell them and their eggs to the family, to the Hurricane store, or to anyone else they chose. Sometimes they sold poultry as well as garden produce and wood from the vast swamps to steamboats plying the adjacent river.[8]

Davis was sensitive to the needs of his workers and regularly rewarded them for unusual achievements, in addition to providing gifts for a birth or wedding or in consolation for a death. Special feasts, often including a whole pig, as well as sweets, coffee, and wine, were supplied for holidays and family celebrations. That the master of Hurricane enjoyed being generous is evident from a reminiscence of one family member:

> There was a little store-room adjoining Mr. Davis's bedroom below stairs, out of which came, in the most astonishing and unexpected variety, candy, negro shoes, field implements, new saddles and bridles, fancy plaid linsey or calico dresses for the negro women who needed consolation for a death in their families, guns and ammunition for hunting, pocket-knives, nails, and screws. This little closet was an ark, of which Mr. J. E. Davis kept the key, and made provision for the accidental needs of "each one after his kind."[9]

By providing such benefits in addition to comfortable housing and generous supplies of food and clothing Joseph Davis hoped to win the cooperation of his slaves, thereby making the plantation both more profitable and more pleasant. Unlike most slaveholders, Davis respected his bondsmen as people very much like whites. From his earliest recollections of the log cabin in Georgia, where his mother and the slave Winny cared for him interchangeably, he had considered blacks to be human beings, in contrast with the dreaded Indians. It was natural for him to adopt Robert Owen's method of rational treatment, allowing his workers to maintain their dignity. As his brother said, Joseph had higher hopes for the slaves' "moral and mental elevation" than did "most men of his experience." He expected them to work hard for their own benefit as well as his, and he was quick to commend and encourage those who performed well.[10]

Davis's benevolent management methods seemed amply vindicated by the example of his most able slave, Benjamin Montgomery, who seized the opportunities Davis provided and became an invaluable assistant as well as confidant and companion to his master. Born in Virginia in 1819, the brilliant Montgomery learned to read and write along with his young master. Each afternoon the slave persuaded the white boy to teach him the letters and words learned that morning. For unknown reasons, this partnership ended abruptly in 1836, when Ben was sold to a trader who marched him overland to the busy slave market in Natchez. It was a boom period for slave trading in the area; in the three years from 1834 to 1837 the slave population of Mississippi more than doubled, from 70,000 to 160,000, at an average price of $1,000 each. In 1836 Ben Montgomery was one of some twenty slaves that Joseph Davis brought from the Natchez market to the expanding plantation at Davis Bend.[11]

The seventeen-year-old slave bitterly resented this abrupt change from Virginia town life to the isolation of Hurricane, where he was a stranger in a large slave community, so he ran away. After quickly recovering the unhappy youth, Davis applied Robert Owen's rational approach and, instead of punishing him, "inquired closely into the cause of his dissatisfaction." Perhaps recognizing his great potential, Davis explained to the lad the many opportunities available at Hurricane and challenged him to take advantage of them. As a result of this unusual conference, Montgomery's son later reported, the master and the young slave "reached a mutual understanding and established a mutual confidence which time only served to strengthen through their long and eventful connection."[12]

Davis's confidence was amply justified. With access to the large Hurricane library, Ben improved his literary skills and was soon copying letters and legal briefs as the office clerk. He learned to survey land to plan the construction of the levees essential for flood protection on Davis Bend. He drew architectural plans and participated in the construction of several buildings, including the elaborate garden cottage. He also became an adept mechanic and was soon maintaining the complex and failure-prone steam engine that powered the gin and mills. In the late 1850s, Ben invented a boat propeller that promised to be an improvement on the paddle wheels used on river steamboats. As Davis declared, he had "few Superiors as a Machinist."[13]

But Montgomery's greatest talent proved to be in the realm of business. In 1842 he established a store on the plantation, selling dry goods and staple items to the slaves in exchange for the wood, chickens, eggs, and vegetables they produced on their own time. After Davis guaranteed his first consignment of goods, Montgomery maintained his own line of credit with New Orleans wholesalers. His store proved popular with both blacks and whites because it saved the slaves a costly trip off the peninsula and allowed the whites to purchase items without waiting for the next trip to Vicksburg or Natchez. One woman from the mansion charged $1,000 worth of goods in a single year. Soon Montgomery began marketing surplus fruit from the orchard and acting as Davis's agent in purchasing supplies and shipping the huge cotton crop. In time, he became the business agent for the entire plantation, relieving his master of much of the routine work.[14]

Davis was delighted with Montgomery's progress and encouraged him to undertake new challenges. As an avid reader himself, the master guided Ben's systematic journey through his library, which was filled with works of political theory and philosophy. As Ben finished each book in his spare time, the two men would discuss it in light of other reading and the current scene. Since Davis was himself self-taught, he considered this the proper way to educate his pupil. Their erudite discussions late in the evening would have shocked many racist planters, who denigrated the slaves' intelligence while living in fear that they might revolt. Since it was against the law to teach bondsmen to read and write, one can only imagine what his neighbors would have thought of Davis introducing Montgomery to the revolutionary theories of Thomas Paine and Thomas Jefferson. It seems probable that Davis kept quiet about this part of Montgomery's education, while openly praising his mechanical and managerial skills.

With profits from his business ventures Ben was soon able to construct a building at the landing to house his store and living quarters for his family. At Christmas in 1840 he married Mary Lewis, literate daughter of the plantation's skilled wheelwright. Although only eighteen at the time of her marriage, Mary was a very capable wife who provided the warmth and stability Ben needed in his adjustment to Hurricane. The income from the store allowed Mary to pay her master the equivalent of her worth as a field hand so that she could remain at home caring for the four children born to the couple by 1850. Although she accepted some sewing jobs for the white women and helped Ben in the store when needed, Mary regarded the rearing of her children as her primary responsibility.[15]

By permitting these able slaves to live very much as did white middle-class storekeepers and encouraging them to educate their children, Davis enjoyed the advantage of having a reliable business manager who could not leave his employ. Ben Montgomery, who read current newspapers and journals and traveled to Vicksburg and New Orleans on business, understood full well the advantages of his situation and never again tried to escape. Master and slave shared a mutual respect and companionship that made life on the plantation more pleasant for both. Davis's enlightened slave management policies paid unexpected dividends after the Civil War, when the Montgomery family became the breadwinners for their former master and his relatives. Although Joseph Davis could not have foreseen this boon, he realized the rewards of greater productivity from his work force under his humane system.

Despite the harmony and productivity at Hurricane, Davis recognized the potential for injustice inherent in the slave system, and he never accepted it as ideal. Isaiah Montgomery reported in later years that Davis's slaves knew that he "considered slavery an evil that was a vexing problem to get rid of." He pondered various possible alternatives without finding a satisfactory solution.[16]

Although he was too far away to be an active member, Davis may have sympathized with the men in Natchez who organized the Mississippi Colonization Society in 1831. His friend Stephen Duncan served as its president, overseeing collection of donations totaling $100,000 in the first three years. The society sent more than 570 former slaves to Liberia, but by 1837, as the South's commitment to slavery hardened, the Mississippi colonization movement lost its popularity and effectiveness. If Davis had seen this as a possible means of ending the peculiar institution, he must have been disappointed.[17]

Joseph Davis, always a practical man, may well have been suspicious of colonization as a solution to slavery. He certainly knew about Isaac Ross, a wealthy planter whose plantation lay between Hurricane and Natchez, because Ross's daughter Margaret was the wife of Davis's former law partner, Thomas B. Reed. Ross was a dedicated member of the colonization society and upon his death in 1836 wanted his slaves to be given the choice of being sold or sent to Liberia as freedmen. Mrs. Reed tried to fulfill her father's wishes, but the other heirs brought suit to break the will. During almost twelve years of litigation, the restless slaves attempted an insurrection, which aroused a great deal of opposition in the white community. Eventually, more than 250 former Ross bondsmen were sent to Africa, the last few surreptitiously.

After the war, Davis claimed that he had wanted to free his slaves for twenty years but could think of no adequate way of guaranteeing their welfare. However he must have had very mixed feelings concerning the institution that made his prosperity possible. In 1840 he wrote his brother indignantly about a meeting he attended in Lexington, Kentucky, where Cassius Clay expressed hostility to slaveowners. The master of Hurricane clearly abhorred abolitionists and saw them as a threat to his way of life. Yet he never accepted the views expressed by his brother Jefferson and most other southern leaders that slavery was a positive good, "ordered of Divine Providence for the benefit of both races involved." His deep concern for his former slaves after the war demonstrated his sincere attachment to them. This dilemma between his anxiety for the welfare of fellow humans and his determination to achieve economic and social status must have tarnished somewhat the satisfaction he felt in the success of the plantation.[18]

The even tenor of plantation life was punctuated by seasonal crises that required maximum effort by community residents for the benefit of all. Harvest season frequently brought such demands since there was some urgency about picking a large cotton crop before bad weather set in. A holiday atmosphere with various incentive programs and competitions between gangs encouraged field hands to give their best efforts to this task.

Even longer hours and harder work were required to meet the ominous menace of floods that threatened the very existence of the plantation every few years. To deal with this problem, Joseph Davis had constructed and constantly sought to improve an elaborate system of levees around his Davis Bend property. Although he considered such protection essential to his planting enterprise, he regarded with suspicion any effort of the government to intervene in the process. Not all his neighbors shared this view. In February 1846, John Henderson, a plantation owner on the Mississippi north of Davis Bend, persuaded James E. Sharkey, the Whig representative from Warren County in the state legislature, to propose flood control measures for his area. As a result, the legislature passed a law providing for the erection and maintenance of levees all along the river in Warren County at the expense of the property owners. Location of the levees and the tax assessment deemed necessary to build and maintain them were to be determined by three levee inspectors and the county board of police.

In November 1846, two of these inspectors, John Henderson and Rice C. Ballard, another wealthy planter, who owned Warren County bottomland, examined the existing levees on Davis Bend and agreed that they provided adequate protection. In January 1847, however, Joseph Davis was officially notified that he must pay one dollar per acre for 1,796 acres of backland that the inspectors claimed would be protected by a levee to be built upstream. Davis was further warned that in case of nonpayment his land would be sold at auction. As a staunch believer in self-help and minimal government, Davis was infuriated, the more so because of the highhanded way in which the matter was handled. Within three weeks he had filed a bill of complaint against the county sheriff (who was also the tax collector) and the levee commissioners. He contended that his land had been improperly inspected because only two of the required three inspectors were present, that he was allowed no appeal of the commissioners' decision, that instead of protecting his property, the proposed levees would cause more flooding on Davis Bend, and finally that the law was a perversion of the taxing power of the government. By this time he had discovered that both Henderson and Sharkey would benefit by the new levee, whereas those at Davis Bend, who were paying for it, would probably suffer increased inundation.[19]

The case worked its way through the courts for the next eight years, during which time friends of Joseph Davis in the state legislature passed another law specifically exempting the lands at Davis Bend from the provisions of the 1846 levee act. By 1851 the chancery court had enjoined both collection of the tax and construction of the levee. Two years later, it decided the case in Davis's favor, a decision that was upheld by the state supreme court in 1856. But the court considered only the question of the absence of one of the inspectors, which it ruled crucial, and did not address the broader question of abuse of the taxing power.[20]

Davis had recourse to the law whenever he deemed it necessary, but if the courts moved too slowly he did not hesitate to take direct action to protect his vital interests. For example, in 1850 he discovered a group of hired hands busily digging a trench across the narrow neck of land connecting the peninsula of Davis Bend to the mainland. Although it was on the property of his neighbors Henry Turner and John Quitman, Davis recognized that this ditch would act as a cutoff, rechanneling the Mississippi River so that it would no longer flow around the peninsula. After fruitless protests to the landowners, Davis brought suit to stop this activity, claiming that it was instigated by steamboat owners who sought to shorten the river and by landowners above the Bend who thought it would deepen the channel and thus help protect them from overflow. But he correctly pointed out that it would cause great flood damage to landowners below the cutoff. He would suffer most because, he predicted, his plantation would be left on a lake some six or seven miles from the navigable river. Davis maintained that he had asked Turner and

Quitman to make the workers stop but with no success, so he requested a restraining order to halt the work.

The records are incomplete so it is impossible to determine the outcome of the court case. Davis withdrew his charges against some of the group he had named, including John Henderson, but a letter from his brother Jefferson many years later indicates that the two Davises took matters into their own hands when court action proved insufficient. Jefferson Davis wrote, "I presume I was the only person in the Confederacy who had ever armed and led negroes against white men, they were the slaves of my Brother and myself and the movement was against a band who were paid and employed secretly to make a Cutoff behind our plantations." Apparently the threat of the armed group halted the digging. The river continued to flow by the Davis plantations until 1867, when a ditch deepened by the Yankees for defense channeled the water away just as Joseph Davis had feared it would.[21]

Although the prosperity of the plantation must have been very gratifying to Joseph Davis, its remoteness precluded extensive social contact. Like most of those bred on the lonely frontier, Davis valued interaction with others, and he undoubtedly missed the informal encounters with a variety of people that he had enjoyed in Natchez. At first, he tried to continue his law practice by taking on a few clients in Vicksburg, but the difficulty of commuting from Davis Bend via infrequent steamboats or over often impassable roads soon forced him to abandon the attempt. Although he continued periodic visits to Natchez and Vicksburg, he had to rely on his family and occasional visitors for daily companionship.

His wife, Eliza, was always devoted to him, but her personality and her chronic ill health made her an inadequate companion. Never one to minimize her symptoms, she tended to complain incessantly and to predict her imminent demise. She was very fond of children, and, as the years passed without any of her own, she eagerly took in an array of homeless tots. These adoptions always met with her husband's hearty approval for he, too, loved playing with the children. Eliza enjoyed making pretty clothes for these youngsters as well as other members of the family, and she proved a capable supervisor of the household slaves. But her favorite recreation was planning and developing the beautiful Hurricane garden. This was her special realm, and she usually took each guest on a tour of it. In 1845 a chance visitor described Mrs. Davis as "a tall, black-eyed lady in black," who hospitably chatted with him and his companion while showing them the garden until the return of Mr. Davis, "a little, oldish man, twenty years at least older than madame." (At that time Davis was sixty-one and Eliza thirty-four.) Educated in the fashion of genteel women of her day, she wrote flowery letters and read novels such as Benjamin Disraeli's *Sybil* and Emilie Carlen's *The Rose of Thistle Island,* which she then passed on to other women of the family. Although she was intelligent, her husband would not expect to find an intellectual partner in Eliza, and like most other women she knew, it would never have occurred to her to discuss history or political theory with him.[22]

Davis's daughters also provided inadequate companionship for their father. Florida, who was a few months older than her stepmother, remained at home only three years after their move to Hurricane. In October 1830 she married David McCaleb, whose father was a prosperous landholder in Claiborne, Washington, and Warren counties. He gave the couple a plantation called Diamond Place located on the Mississippi a few miles north of Davis Bend. Evidently young McCaleb was a poor manager, for he fell into debt, and in 1846 Joseph Davis bought Diamond Place at a trustees sale, allowing Florida and her husband to continue operating it. The next year McCaleb died suddenly, but Florida continued to live on the place. As a widow, she suffered from a number of ailments that some relatives deemed imaginary. One "remarkably complaisant" doctor prescribed a dangerous mixture of "aqua vite, arsenic, morphene [and] laudanum" that only worsened her condition. Fortunately, her brother-in-law, also a physician, happened to visit and effected a cure by telling her to throw away the drugs and get out of bed. Less than a year later, Florida married Edmund Laughlin, younger member of the firm that served as her father's factors in New Orleans. The couple continued to live at Diamond Place, trying to work out McCaleb's indebtedness.[23]

Like her stepmother, Florida remained childless. Soon after her first marriage, she adopted a little girl, Julia Lyons, whom she sent to the same convent school in New Orleans that her sister and perhaps she had attended. Julia later married William Porterfield, an alcoholic Irishman more than twenty years her senior, who had developed a prosperous insurance and steamboat business in Vicksburg. Florida and Laughlin adopted his brother's four children after they were orphaned. Florida, whose favorite pastimes were reading French novels and playing the guitar, was a generous, self-effacing woman who tried hard to please. She may have been embarrassed by her illegitimate birth; in a letter to her Uncle Jefferson, her friend since their school days, she described herself as "the very type of obscurity whose life has been but a tissue of misfortune from my very birth, and that the greatest." Although he tried to be fair to her, Joseph Davis was never especially fond of Florida.[24]

Mary Lucinda, Davis's second daughter, had a sunny disposition that made her a favorite with everyone. She wanted to stay in the New Orleans convent where she was educated. However, her father not only refused to let her become a nun but would not let her join the Catholic church. With no apparent rancor, she dutifully returned to Hurricane and busied herself with gardening, sewing, and helping her family. Her stepmother claimed, "She is much company for us dividing her time between Florida and Myself." Mary was devoted to Florida, five years her elder, whom she called "Sister," while always referring to her younger sibling as "Carrie."[25]

In 1838, when Mary was twenty-one, she married Dr. Charles J. Mitchell and accompanied him to Paris, where he studied surgery for two years. During their stay in France, Mary learned a great deal, not only from her studies of French literature with a tutor but also from observing life in that sophisticated capital. Although receptive to new ideas in fashions of clothing, food, and housekeeping, she missed family and friends and the opportunity to ride her favorite horse over the Mississippi countryside. This daughter of the American frontier was defensively nationalistic in conversation with French acquaintances and felt no regret at leaving the excitement of Paris in 1840. She was especially eager to return home to introduce the family to her new son, Joseph Davis Mitchell, born the previous year. Her tales of life in a foreign land must have been especially welcome to her father.

After the birth of a daughter, Mary Elizabeth, and another son, Hugh, Dr. Mitchell succumbed to the mania for cotton cultivation. He gave up his medical practice in Vicksburg and began developing a plantation across the river in Louisiana. Joseph Davis gave the couple the land and a number of slaves. Mary and the children stayed at Hurricane during the months their house was under construction, but she was not destined to enjoy a long life on the new place. She suffered from poor health after Hugh's birth in 1843, and her condition worsened. Despite her husband's efforts and a therapeutic trip to Cuba, she died in 1846. In accordance with her last wishes, the three small children were raised by her father and stepmother.[26]

Caroline, Joseph Davis's youngest daughter, was the prettiest and the most difficult of the three. Only four years old when her father married and brought her to Hurricane, she never developed any affection for her stepmother or sisters and seemed to care for no one but Davis. Always unruly, she resisted various plans for her education and alienated much of the extended family. When she was ten, she spent several months in Woodville with her grandmother Jane Davis, sharing classes with orphaned cousins Ellen and Jane, who lived there. When her stepmother visited them, she reported that Caroline was "a trouble to Mother" and suggested that she might be sent to a new girls' boarding school in Clinton. Seven years later, Caroline was so discontented at school in Nazareth, Kentucky, that she insisted on leaving with her parents before completing final examinations. In a letter to her uncle, she said she wanted to go to school in the North for two years, adding that when she returned, "perhaps I will not make my friends ashamed." She seemed confused and unhappy, stating, "O! Uncle you cannot know how much I have wished to get in some little place to my self away from the noise & bustle of the world."[27]

In 1842, when she was nineteen, the beautiful Caroline married Thomas E. Robins, fifteen years her senior, who was a prominent Vicksburg resident and a friend of her father and her Uncle Jefferson. Unfortunately, Robins was incapable of providing the stability his bride needed. He served as an officer of the Commercial and Railroad Bank and responded to accusations that he embezzled funds by challenging his accusers to duels, of which he fought several, both before and after his marriage. Despite a rather shady reputation, he prospered financially for a time, building a spectacular mansion in Vicksburg that came to be called the Castle. Throughout the 1840s he was active in Democratic politics along with the Davis brothers. Joseph Davis gave him and Caroline a plantation adjacent to her sister's on Brushy Bayou in Louisiana, but they failed to develop it. During this period, Caroline bore two sons, Jack and Joseph, both of whom died in infancy and were buried at Hurricane. Robins made frequent trips abroad seeking to improve his fortunes, but by 1849 he was bankrupt. The next year he returned to his family home in New York, where he died. A Vicksburg newspaper reported that "he was insane at the time of his death, as he had been for some time previous." This unfortunate marriage, which must have caused Davis considerable concern, did nothing to improve Caroline's fragile mental health.[28]

In 1856, after an unhappy six years' residence in her father's home, Caroline married Abraham F. Leonard and moved to Norfolk, Virginia, where he was a successful newspaper editor. Although it was said that she remained beautiful, with dark, expressive eyes and jet-black hair, Caroline never found the stability or happiness she sought. After her second husband's death in 1870 from acute alcoholism, which one family member attributed to the difficulties of living with her, she spent her old age in poverty in a Virginia insane asylum. Joseph Davis was never able to establish a satisfactory relationship with his troubled youngest daughter.[29]

During the 1840s, Joseph and Eliza Davis added several adopted children to the Hurricane household. The year before Mary's death left them with her three little ones, the Davises had taken in Joseph Davis Nicholson, the infant son of Jane Nicholson, possibly a distant cousin, who died at Hurricane. Her husband, who lived on Davis Bend, died just a year after his wife, and their son grew up at Hurricane. Some years earlier, the Davises had invited the widow of Joseph's old mentor Judge William Wallace of Kentucky for an extended visit to the plantation. She was accompanied by her orphaned granddaughter Martha Quarles, whom she was raising. When Mrs. Wallace became ill and died during her visit, the Davises adopted Martha, providing for her education and support throughout most of her life.

In addition to these wards, Davis added an entire family to his household. In 1844 his brother-in-law David Bradford, a lawyer and planter across the river in Madison Parish, Louisiana, was assassinated by an enraged litigant. His widow, Davis's sister Amanda, tried to operate the plantation for the next two years, but by December 1846 she gladly accepted Joseph's offer to move slaves, possessions, and seven of her children to Hurricane. David Bradford's body was exhumed and reinterred in the Hurricane cemetery. The five Bradford girls, ranging from thirteen to twenty-one years of age, added youthful gaiety to the plantation. Along with the Davis daughters and Martha Quarles, they supplied brides for ten elaborate weddings that Eliza happily staged at Hurricane in the antebellum years. The Bradford daughters provided additional supervisors for the younger Davis wards, but the two Bradford boys, aged seven and eleven when they moved in, were often rowdy and undisciplined. No wonder Joseph Davis, now in his sixties, frequently sought refuge in his neoclassical garden cottage, where his office was open to visitors by invitation only.[30]

Although Davis was particularly fond of children, neither they nor the women of the household could provide the intellectual companionship he relished. He found this stimulation most regularly with his youngest brother, Jefferson, who was twenty-three years his junior and much like a favorite son. In 1828 the younger Davis graduated from the United States Military Academy at West Point. For the next seven years he served honorably in the regular army, often on the Northwest frontier, where he was involved in campaigns against the Indians. As early as 1832, he asked Joseph's advice about alternative careers, but he remained in the army until 1835, when he accepted his brother's gift of land adjoining Hurricane at Davis Bend.

The precipitating factor in his decision to change careers was Jefferson's desire to marry Sarah Knox Taylor, daughter of his superior officer, Zachary Taylor. Despite Taylor's objections, they were married at her aunt's home in Kentucky. Shortly afterward, in June 1835, the newlyweds arrived at Davis Bend. There Jefferson and a small slave force, bought with a loan from his brother, began clearing the new plantation he named Brier-field. Neither Jefferson nor his bride was acclimated to the South, and by September both had severe cases of malaria from which Knox soon died. Ill and despondent, young Davis spent several months recuperating in Louisiana and Cuba before returning to the lonely task of planting. For the next few years he worked hard to develop Brierfield into a successful cotton plantation. He lived at Hurricane until he and his capable slave foreman, Jim Pemberton, could design and build a small house on his own land. Even after he moved, the Davis brothers continued to spend long hours together riding over their acres or, in the eve-ning, discussing planting, politics, and world affairs in Joseph's office. Jefferson could read and appreciate the works of political philosophy that Joseph cherished. He had much more formal education than his elder brother and undoubtedly contributed new ideas to their discussions. There were evidently few argu-ments because both men were staunch Jeffersonian Democrats who viewed all current political questions in light of their firm belief in strict construction of the Constitution.[31]

The brothers' discussions became less frequent after 1845, when Jefferson entered both politics and a second marriage, but despite long absences from Davis Bend, he remained Joseph Davis's closest confidant. Jefferson's second wife, Varina Howell, was the daughter of Joseph's good friends from Natchez and had grown up calling her future brother-in-law "Uncle Joe," but their relationship was often a stormy one. Varina, only nineteen at the time of her marriage, was a strong-willed, assertive woman determined to have things her own way. She was unusually in-telligent and far better educated than most women of her time, having been thoroughly tutored in the classics by Judge George Winchester of Natchez. Her quick wit and broad background, as well as a lively interest in current affairs, would seem to have made her a great addition to the limited society available to Joseph Davis. When she was alone on the plantation for long periods while Jefferson was campaigning for office, serving in Washington, or fighting in the Mexican War, Varina spent many evenings with Joseph reading and discussing newspapers and recent additions to the Hurricane library. But there was an underlying tension between the two that precluded true companionship and led to open hostility at times.

It is difficult to pinpoint the cause of the friction between Davis and his much younger sister-in-law. Both were sensitive, highly intelligent people who tended to dominate others. Some historians have attributed their difficulties to the jealousy each felt of the other's influence over Jefferson Davis, but such a monocausal explanation seems to oversimplify two very complex characters. Davis was undoubtedly devoted to his youngest brother and may well have relished Jefferson's political success as a vicarious realization of his own thwarted ambition in politics, but he never tried to dominate the younger man. By the late 1840s Joseph was so secure in his own position, and his relationship with his brother was so different from that of a wife, that it seems unlikely that he would be jealous of Varina.

She may have resented the brothers' close relationship, however. Varina was extremely high-strung and prone to nervous ailments even before her marriage, and her insecurity was probably increased by marriage to a man nearly twenty years her senior who immediately launched a political career that kept him in the public eye. She was required either to spend long periods without him or to move to unfamiliar surroundings where she faced many social obligations. Although at times she rose to the occasion brilliantly, she remained a chronic malcontent whose intolerant plain-spokenness often antagonized those around her. Even her mild-mannered husband, who loved her very much, sometimes found it impossible to live with her. In early 1848, after only three years of marriage, he went to Washington without her because, he told her, "the dread of constant strife was so great." He claimed he left "with body crippled, nerves shattered, and mind depressed" as a result of her behavior, and he warned that her "course if continued would render it impossible for us ever to live together." They reconciled this difference and numerous others during their long marriage, but Varina remained an abrasive person.[32]

Her relations with the women at Hurricane were frequently strained. Joseph's wife, Eliza, was herself a querulous woman with low self-esteem who constantly demanded evidence of affection from family members. She and Varina clashed from the beginning, competing to display the grandest clothes or gardens while each disparaged those of the other. When in residence, Caroline gleefully joined this game, goading Varina about such things as her inadequate wine cellar or the fact that Joseph Davis still held title to Brierfield, thus making Jefferson dependent upon his brother. When Jefferson Davis sought to build a duplex house at Brierfield large enough to accommodate his sister Amanda and her family as well as his own, Varina refused to share her home. In her husband's absence, she and Joseph had what she later termed "quite an angry contest" over her insistence on changing the plans for the kitchen. As on several other occasions, Joseph claimed he was only trying to protect Jefferson from his wife's extravagance.[33]

Petty misunderstandings among the women continued, punctuated by some open breaks. Isolated on the plantation with only mundane duties of household supervision and child care to occupy them, these intelligent women had few outlets but gossip and petty strife. Early in her marriage, Eliza expressed her boredom at Hurricane: "I look forward to change in some form as regards our Mode of living. . . . I am not satisfied." Admitting that she was indolent, she added, "I sometimes feel as if I had no motive for exertion." Her hopes for any drastic change were unrealistic, and like her colleagues she was doomed to live vicariously through her husband, gaining status only through his achievements. Some women sought outlets in religion; Eliza was later confirmed by the Episcopal bishop and seemed to get satisfaction from the clergy's attentions. Amanda and her daughters, who attended a convent school in Kentucky, joined the Roman Catholic church. Varina's energies were often occupied in the Washington social whirl, but whenever she was in residence at Brierfield she seemed antagonistic toward the Hurricane family.[34]

These quarrels distressed Jefferson Davis so acutely that his health was impaired. He was caught between his love for his wife and his loyalty to his fatherly older brother. In 1852 some difficulty arose involving derogatory remarks about the Davises made by Margaret Howell, Varina's mother, on board a steamboat that were overheard and repeated by the troublemaker Caroline. The affair became so serious that Joseph Davis broke off his long friendship with the elder Howells, and there ensued an estrangement from Jefferson and Varina that lasted until 1855. During this time, Jefferson reportedly threatened to sell Brierfield, and Joseph offered to buy it. Joseph changed the terms of his will to ensure that neither Varina nor any of her numerous and chronically impoverished family would inherit any part of his property. Eventually, after causing much pain to both the brothers, the breach was healed and the families resumed friendly contact. However, Varina continued to cherish a hatred for her brother-in-law, which she later asserted arose from some affront he had given her soon after her marriage. She bitterly resented her husband's insistence on naming one of their sons for his brother, and she made a point of telling Joseph of her objections. Many years later, after Joseph Davis's death, Varina claimed that he had offered her expensive gifts and trips to placate her and that she was one of his favorites. She said, "We were isolated from society, congenial in our tastes, both had a keen sense of the ludicrous, and we very often warmed up into confidential talks and conferences, when our interests were so near, and we knew all parties so well. I think he said very often more to me than he did to those who loved him better." But this intermittent companionship was bought at a very dear price. From Joseph's point of view, Varina must have brought more pain than pleasure to Davis Bend.[35]

In addition to the psychological stress caused by family friction, Davis and others at Davis Bend frequently suffered from physical pain and discomfort. Middle-aged when he moved to Hurricane, Joseph Davis experienced a variety of ailments during the next thirty-five years; however, given the unhealthy location of the plantation and the primitive state of medical knowledge, it is surprising that he was in good health most of the time. In 1838 he suffered an unusually long siege of an undiagnosed illness that prompted him to talk of getting his papers in order in preparation for death. Having spent a sickly winter, he took his family to a health resort at Hot Springs, Arkansas, in July. While there, he had a sudden seizure that left him briefly unconscious. He awoke to find the doctors bleeding him so enthusiastically that his daughter said "the loss of blood and its consequent debility kept him confined to his bed for a day or two." Apparently, the attack worried Davis, for Florida continued, "He tries to forget it, or laugh at it but it evidently distresses him." This ailment and his fears were temporary, but Davis continued to suffer the usual bouts of respiratory and digestive illness that plagued everyone. He was fortunate that his was an unusually strong constitution so he did not succumb to the many infections for which there was no remedy. Nor did he contract the major diseases such as cholera or yellow fever that decimated the local population from time to time. Davis even seemed to avoid the debilitating effects of the endemic malaria.[36]

In the dampness of the riverside plantation, Davis received a visit every winter from what he called "my old acquaintance the rheumatism," making it painful to get on or off a horse. And he sometimes had less predictable physical problems. One year a family friend wrote Jefferson about his brother's recent encounter with a mad dog, which observers blamed for "a change in his manner of late; . . . from great vivacity & buoyancy to apparent depression [&] melancholy." The friend enclosed a recipe that he believed to be "an antidote." Such home remedies were probably less dangerous than the drugs prescribed by the poorly trained doctors of the era, who often seemed to do their patients more harm than good. Davis was indeed fortunate to avoid their ministrations.[37]

Other family members did not fare as well. Jefferson Davis was frequently ill even as a young soldier on the frontier. He suffered a painful foot wound in the Mexican War, and while serving in the government in Washington he sometimes spent weeks at a time too ill to leave his house. As a result of one infection, he lost the sight in one eye. Jefferson's health was a cause of great concern to his family.

Eliza was more often ill than well; she suffered from chest pains at the slightest exertion and frequently complained of nervous attacks. The rest of the females in the family added to the common problems the very real hazards of childbirth and resulting complications. After the birth of her last child, Joseph's daughter Mary Mitchell hemorrhaged intermittently for many months until she died. Jefferson's wife, Varina, was so ill during one of her pregnancies that she expected to die when the baby was born. Many infants failed to survive the crucial first year, and if they managed to do so, often succumbed to dysentery as toddlers. The older children, too, had to make their way through childhood diseases as well as adult ones without benefit of miracle drugs. The course of treatment regularly prescribed by physicians was often harmful and provided still another hazard for nineteenth-century patients.[38]

Death was very familiar to everyone in that nineteenth-century society, black and white, rich and poor. Partings tended to be sentimentally affectionate because the participants realized there was a good possibility they would never see each other alive again. In the eight-year period from 1844 to 1852, Joseph Davis lost twelve members of his family, eight of whom died at Hurricane. The deceased included his mother, a daughter, three grandsons, a brother-in-law, two sons-in-law, a niece, a nephew, and two cousins. They ranged in age from eighty-four-year-old Jane Cook Davis to little Joseph Davis Robins, who was less than a year old, but most were in the generation just younger than Joseph Davis. No wonder the master of Hurricane was acutely aware that his days were numbered.

The most painful loss for Davis was probably that of his five-year-old grandson Hugh Mitchell, who died after a horseback riding accident. The youngest of the three children whom Mary had left for her father to raise, Hugh had spent his whole life at Hurricane and was especially dear to his grandfather. Some months after his death, Davis wrote Dr. Mitchell that "the voices of the children are painful, suddenly recalling my lost boy," and familiar objects associated with him constantly evoked fond memories. Davis went on, "I have suffered other afflictions, other hopes have been blighted, but whether from the time of life when fewer objects engage my attention and care, or whether from my more intimate association with him I know not, but nothing has weighed down my spirit like this."[39]

In an effort to avoid the life-threatening diseases so common in summer and early fall, prosperous southerners often gathered at health resorts usually located where natural springs allowed them to drink and bathe in the water. Joseph Davis was reluctant to leave the responsibilities of his bustling plantation, but Ben Montgomery's growing competence combined with the threat of illness or death for himself and family often persuaded him to follow the crowd to the watering places. As late as 1848, however, he was still hesitant about leaving home. In April, a few months before he was elected president, Zachary Taylor visited his friends at Hurricane. He promptly wrote to Jefferson noting Joseph's poor health, which he attributed to overwork.

Conceding that Davis had built "a little paradis [sic] & surrounded it with every comfort & I may say luxury," Taylor insisted "he ought now to think more about the preservation of his health than making cotton & corn."[40]

Conditions at the spas often provided neither health nor comfort. In 1838 Florida Davis McCaleb wrote her uncle of her discomfort and boredom during a family stay at Hot Springs, Arkansas. She disliked the "'out-cast humans'" who "infested" the resort, forcing her to read or play her guitar shut up "in a very hot room." She complained about the food and declared, "We have existed here for four weeks, and . . . I [am] astonished that I still survive." In the 1850s the Davises and many of their friends and relatives regularly visited Cooper's Well near Jackson, Mississippi, although conditions there were scarcely better. One summer Varina declined to accompany the family because she understood their discomfort. As she told her mother, "At one time they had Martha and her two children, Sister Eliza and her two, Cousin Harriet, and her one, Sister Amanda, and Betty, and Brother Joe in two small rooms . . . and all cross as bears." She concluded, "All the family have been sick since they went out, and I expect they are uncomfortable enough." Two months later, after their return to Hurricane, Eliza reported, "Our departure was hastened as every change in the weather in the cabin was felt, being without a fire place . . . home here is certainly more pleasant." She noted that she was slowly recovering from "a severe attack of Bronchitis." The primary benefits from these pilgrimages to health resorts may have been social and psychological rather than physical.[41]

Whether for improved health, business, politics, or pure recreation, Joseph Davis sometimes took his family on extended summer trips. Often these jaunts served several purposes. For example, after their sojourn at the spa in Hot Springs, Arkansas, in 1838 the Davises traveled on to Kentucky, where they visited Louisville, Bardstown, Harrodsburg, and Lexington. While in the latter city Davis shopped around for the lowest prices on "linsey &c" for the slaves and "Castings & baging [sic] & rope" for ginning cotton. He also found time for "a ride of 8 miles on a very warm day" to visit the stables that housed some of the finest horses in the Blue Grass country; there he contracted to buy a handsome colt. The journey ended in St. Louis, where Davis completed his purchases for the plantation, returning home by steamboat after an absence of almost three months. In every town they visited the Davises contacted old friends, and along the way they made new ones so that they were invited to many social functions.

Two years later, in 1840, Davis again took some of the family through Kentucky on the way to White Sulphur Springs in Virginia (now West Virginia). After a sojourn at this health resort, the Davises went on to New York. This was an election year, and Davis reported that he "heard nothing [but] a continual din of Politicks" expounded by "Clerks without employment[,] Speculators without Capital[,] & Lawyers without business." The variety of their modes of transportation is indicated by his statement that "not a Steam Boat, Stage, rail Car, or bar room but rings with" impassioned political harangues. Although he claimed to be disgusted by these discussions, he probably relished the chance to expound his firmly held beliefs to a wide variety of people.[42]

When Jefferson Davis was in Washington, first as congressman, then as senator, and later as secretary of war, Joseph Davis sometimes included a visit with him and his family in the summer itinerary. For example, in 1848, Joseph and Eliza escorted Varina Davis back to Washington, where they spent several weeks before going on to the Democratic national convention in Baltimore to which Joseph was a delegate. The Joseph Davises then returned to Mississippi by way of a spa in Virginia. In 1856, as part of the reconciliation after the long breach between their families, Joseph and Eliza and several young wards visited Jefferson and Varina and their baby daughter at the Redwood, Maryland, resort where they were spending the summer.[43]

Although methods of transportation improved over the years and were better in the 1850s than when Joseph Davis and the Howells made their trip to West Point and New York in 1825, travel remained an arduous undertaking fraught with many hazards. Stagecoach or horse-drawn carriage was the least comfortable mode of transport because of the dreadful condition of most roads. In Mississippi the shortage of natural stone for road building meant that good thoroughfares must be constructed from wooden planks, a costly process undertaken by private capital in only those few places where tolls might repay the expense. For example, in the early 1850s a plank road was built from Yazoo City to Benton, Mississippi, at a cost of $4,000 a mile. Although annual tolls provided 25 percent of the capital, it was impossible to find enough investors to finance a significant portion of the state's roads. Most received only minimum attention from adjacent property owners whose slaves worked on them briefly each year. In 1833 Joseph Davis was named overseer of the road on Davis Bend and found it very difficult to get his neighbors to help work on it when the surface was dry enough. He reported that a declining number of slaves were assigned to the job as the days passed because "many of the hands were said to [be] sick or unfit for duty." He concluded that it would take more energy "at a more favorable season" before the road "may be rendered passable." As a result of such problems, the roads were rough in dry weather and impassable when it rained. Since similar conditions prevailed in other states, the Davises avoided overland stage journeys whenever possible.

As the antebellum years passed, railroads became a more common alternative mode of travel. The line from Vicksburg to Jackson was the most traveled in Mississippi, and Joseph Davis used it regularly. In the Northeast the Davis family frequently traveled the more numerous and convenient rail lines. By 1860 Davis was able to take his family by train from a remote spring in the western Virginia mountains to Knoxville and perhaps on to Jackson and Vicksburg, although he told his brother they might "take a Boat at Memphis." Railroad travel was dirty and dangerous, accidents were frequent, and the cars were often crowded with rowdies who were offensive to ladies. Davis, like most planters, always regarded railroads as merely auxiliary to river traffic.[44]

Whenever possible, Davis traveled by steamboat, which was much more comfortable than stagecoach or train. The large Mississippi packets had spacious main cabins heated by fires on cool days where one could sit in an easy chair, eat palatable meals, move about, and make new friends or visit with old ones. One historian has described these antebellum boats as "the chief meeting place of the planters of the lower Mississippi Valley." Here they could discuss without interruption such vital topics as politics, the price of slaves, cotton, or land, and the latest agricultural methods. In later years the steamers provided sleeping accommodations; for example, the *General Quitman* advertised in 1859 that it contained "fifty staterooms, all furnished in the best possible style." The elegant main cabin, "the highest and best ventilated on the river," was carpeted "with the richest and most costly velvet carpets." The larger boats included a separate lounge where the women could enjoy each others' company safe from the rowdy drunkenness, profanity, and errant tobacco juice all too common among the men.[45]

Probably the chief disadvantage of river travel was the irregularity of the boats' schedules, which meant that passengers must remain on or near the dock with baggage packed for indefinite periods. Only the smaller packets stopped at Davis Bend, and they made very slow progress up or down the river, stopping to load or unload freight and passengers at every plantation landing or small village. Travel was especially slow during the fall and winter months, when the boats stopped to load the cotton harvest bound for New Orleans markets. These smaller craft lacked the luxuries of large steamboats and could be uncomfortably hot and crowded. When the Davises were going as far as Louisville, St. Louis, or New Orleans, they usually took a local boat up to Vicksburg and then transferred to one of the floating palaces that made fewer stops.

River travel on the Mississippi was not without its dangers. When fog or rain seriously obscured visibility, boats tied up for several hours until the pilot could see the narrow channel well enough to avoid dangerous obstacles. Sudden, dramatic accidents were not unusual, with steamboats burning and sinking, often after disastrous explosions. Foolhardy captains racing other boats or their own speed records and urged on by eager passengers sometimes overloaded the pressure on the boiler after soldering shut the safety valve. In the resultant explosion, according to one historian, "Flying wreckage, floods of steam, and scalding water killed and maimed people by the hundreds." In 1837 Lucinda Stamps, Davis's sister, was still shaken a week after witnessing the burning and sinking of the steamboat *Ben Sherrod* immediately opposite their plantation above Fort Adams, Mississippi. The vessel had been racing another steamer from New Orleans when it caught fire and sank. Despite the rescue efforts of William Stamps and his neighbors, more than 200 passengers died. Such disasters occurred more frequently as river traffic increased. It has been estimated that one-third of all steamboats built before the middle of the nineteenth century were lost in accidents. In 1850 alone, fifty-nine of these vessels were destroyed on the Mississippi and its tributaries with a loss of 249 lives. Despite these harrowing statistics, Joseph Davis did not hesitate to take his family on board for long trips each year. He may have rationalized that the health hazards at home were at least as great, and travel was much more exciting.[46]

In 1859 Davis undertook the most extensive trip of his life. Despite the unusually damaging floods that swept Davis Bend that spring, the family left Hurricane in late May. They traveled first to Washington, D.C., for a visit with Jefferson's family, which had recently been increased by the birth of a third child, named Joseph over Varina's objections. Eliza was completely charmed by her husband's namesake, and Joseph offered to provide a nursemaid if Varina would bring her three children and join his party for the rest of their journey. After Varina declined this invitation, the Joseph Davis entourage moved on to Philadelphia and Easton, Pennsylvania, where they visited a Bradford niece and her family. Then they moved on to New York, staying in a hotel which Davis deemed to be "of more pretention than merits." From here he made arrangements for their voyage to Europe. Jefferson had already written to the U.S. consul in London asking his assistance in selecting routes and places to visit. On the eve of their departure, Joseph wrote his brother, "I feel so much the necessity of being at home that if I were to consult my judgment & feeling should give up the voyage." But the next day, June 22, 1859, he sailed aboard the steamer *Africa,* accompanied by Eliza, grandchildren Lise and Joe Mitchell, now seventeen and twenty years old, Mary Van Benthuysen, Eliza's young niece, and three servants.[47]

After landing at Liverpool, the party spent a few days in England before crossing to Dublin. Eliza and the young people were fascinated by their visits to the Zoological Gardens and Dublin Castle, where all were impressed by the review of five thousand troops, "artillery, cavalry & Infantry," that they and crowds of other people witnessed on a huge plain. Although Joseph had been eager to visit Ireland, his wife reported that he was equally anxious to leave, being "restless and dissatisfied." Part of his discontent stemmed from problems getting money exchanged at what he considered a fair rate. Eliza noted, "Travelling is more expensive than I thought—Our ordinary expenses average five pounds daily." She found this exorbitant for such simple living since they seldom had wine, but she added that their bills were increased by their consumption of fresh fruit, especially the "fine strawberries" they found so tempting.[48]

They traveled by comfortable first-class rail carriage through lovely Irish scenery to Belfast and on to Scotland. Arriving in Glasgow on July 14, Davis was disappointed to be unable to recall the married name of an old female friend from Natchez who lived there. Eliza commented that her husband should have married this "tall handsome girl" so that he might have had "a family & a wife with health & every good quality." Joseph seemed to be restless in Scotland, too, for his wife noted that unlike the rest of them, "The news of the day interests him more than sight seeing." In London, however, he was fascinated with the Crystal Palace, which Eliza deemed "worth a visit daily for a week." Here "Mr. Davis was interested in all that he saw." They stayed in small private hotels that had no public rooms where the Davises could meet people, and Eliza felt that this was a major cause of her husband's discontent. Like most rural dwellers, the Davises considered social contacts the most valuable part of any vacation. Nevertheless, in London they received a few calls from American acquaintances and made new friends who advised them about places to see and to shop there and at their next stop.[49]

From England the Davis party crossed to the Continent for a few weeks in Paris before going on to Brussels. In Switzerland Davis, a firm believer in the therapeutic value of cold water, was so pleased by the hydrotherapy treatments that he persuaded his Swiss doctor to return with him to Hurricane. There, while his wife tutored the children in French, the doctor set up a "Water Cure Hospital" with steam-driven machinery that accommodated slaves as well as the white residents. Eliza brought back carpets, furniture, and exotic plants for the garden, while the girls concentrated on jewelry and clothing. Davis had considered leaving Joe Mitchell in Europe to study, but his health seemed too delicate so the entire family returned home in early October. Although Joseph Davis was remarkably healthy and active for a man of seventy-five and he enjoyed the new ideas and broadened horizons he had gained from the trip, he must have been happy to retire to Hurricane again after such a long absence.[50]

Whether at home at Hurricane or on one of his trips, Davis's greatest interest aside from his planting enterprise was politics. Like many of his contemporaries in that pretelevision, presports era, he followed the intricacies of local, state, and national politics with unwavering attentiveness. As one relative later noted, "Joseph Davis was a man of great versatility of mind, a student of governmental law, [who] took an intense interest in the movements of the great political parties of the day." He kept abreast of national issues by subscriptions to Richmond, Charleston, and New Orleans newspapers and relied on the London *Times* for information on world affairs. A patriot who "read and almost committed to memory" the Constitution, *The Federalist,* and *Elliot's Debates,* Davis remained a staunch Jeffersonian Democrat, but he made up his own mind on each issue independent of party allegiance and sometimes altered his stand over the years. For example, in 1831 he joined with some Natchez friends in signing a resolution favoring the tariff and condemning nullification. This group later formed the nucleus of the new Whig party in Mississippi, but Davis soon broke with them politically and by 1842 was denouncing all tariffs. Nevertheless, he maintained his friendship with fellow planters, most of whom remained Whigs. Davis was a soft-spoken man, described as "habitually mild, though keenly, yet good-humoredly, satirical, pointing his arguments usually with some homely anecdotes which generally turned the laugh on his opponent."[51]

Although he had admired Andrew Jackson since his brothers

fought under him at New Orleans in 1815 and like most Mississippians always accorded him unstinting praise for his effective policy of Indian removal, Davis had some reservations about the tide of popular control that seemed to be sweeping the country during the Jacksonian era. In 1832, when the Mississippi legislature scheduled a convention to revise the state constitution which he had helped compose, Davis ran for election as a delegate from Warren County. Although he made numerous stump speeches, he was not surprised to be defeated because he opposed the popular election of judges. As he noted, "The popular Current . . . was for electing every thing." His former Natchez colleague with similar convictions John Quitman won election but was unable to sway the convention even though he warned that popular election of judges "would be dangerous to the extreme, would tend to corruption, and would strike a fatal blow at the independent judiciary." The constitution of 1832 was more democratic than its predecessor of 1817, with fewer property qualifications for voting and more elective offices. In later years both Quitman and Davis admitted that they had been wrong about the dire consequences of such reforms.[52]

Still, Joseph Davis remained concerned about maintaining law and order in a society only beginning to emerge from the frontier phase. During his years on the plantation, Vicksburg became the largest city in Mississippi and the center of economic and political activity for Warren County. In the early 1830s, while he was conducting business and pursuing his limited law practice there, Davis was disturbed by the rowdiness of drunken crowds surrounding the gambling games that flourished both along the riverfront and above in the respectable section of town. He must have sympathized with the public mood of frustration that led to the events of July 1835, when violence erupted between the Vicksburg militia and some gamblers who disrupted their Independence Day banquet. One troublemaker was tarred and feathered immediately, and all gamblers were warned to leave the city by the next day. When five proved re-calcitrant, a vigilante group of militia and leading citizens seized, whipped, and hanged them.

Popular excitement was heightened by rumors of an impend-ing slave insurrection throughout the South linked to white out-laws and northern abolitionists. Although there was never con-crete evidence of such a plot, by mid-July public hysteria resulted in the lynching of twelve whites and many more blacks in Mis-sissippi. Davis never feared violence from his own slaves but the possibility of insurrection nearby must have been a worry, especially since by 1840 slaves made up more than 65 percent of the population of the river counties. Davis always deplored mob violence, whether by whites or blacks, and urged the ne-cessity of due process of law in a civilized society. In 1838, when a respected lawyer presented to the legislature a new di-gest of the laws of Mississippi it had requested, Davis com-mented, "Few have read it, perhaps none and I think it quite probable they will reject it after the labor of four or five years without examination." He regretted that improvements in the law could not be made because "the old Lawyers are opposed to any innovation."[53]

Although by the 1840s most professional gamblers had re-treated to the riverboats, Vicksburg was still plagued by vio-lence. Though willing to overlook drunken street brawls be-tween lower-class rowdies, community leaders were disturbed by disputes among their own members that resulted in deaths. On two consecutive days in May 1844 two duels resulted in the wounding of one man and the death of another, prompting a group of concerned citizens to call a meeting for the purpose of organizing an antidueling society. Both Joseph and Jefferson Davis were interested parties, at least partly because one of the duelists was Joseph's son-in-law Thomas E. Robins. Two years earlier, just a few months before his marriage to Caroline Davis, Robins had challenged the editor of the *Sentinel* for printing an implication that he was a swindler. On this occasion, Joseph Davis had intervened and arbitrated the dispute temporarily. When the editor failed to print an apology as promised, Robins wounded him on the field of honor and the journalist left town. In 1843 and 1844 three editors of the *Sentinel* were involved in fatal fights and two more were to die in later disputes. Most of these affairs involved political disagreements that frequently were settled not by ritualized duels but by shots from ambush.

It was against this background that leading men of the community met in 1844 and drew up resolutions creating the Mississippi Antidueling Society, whose members were pledged not only to forego all violence themselves but to endeavor to prevent such combat among their associates. According to the Democratic *Sentinel,* all those who drafted and signed these resolves were Whigs, whom the paper characterized as cowards. Among those objecting to their action were Colonel Robins, Captain Jefferson Davis, and "the main speaker, J. E. Davis, Esq." After a long speech of explanation, Jefferson Davis offered some counterproposals to the total ban on dueling. He attacked the practices of carrying concealed weapons and of engaging in "public broils and street rencontres," which endangered the lives of peaceful citizens and the reputation of the city. Although all such disputes should be discouraged, he claimed that dueling provided a means of last resort of regulating conflicts with fairness and equality. Joseph Davis, who had opposed outlawing duels since the state constitutional convention in 1817, asserted that forty years of experience had convinced him that "the responsibility of the duel could not now be abolished" without Vicksburg becoming "the abode of those closely approximating to highwaymen." Although their proposals were voted down and the original charter adopted, this may have resulted more from partisan politics than from the substance of the arguments presented. The *Sentinel* noted that "but one democrat" voted with the Whigs.[54]

A recent historian has asserted that duels provided structure and ritual for southern combat: "Referees assured the fairness of the fight and witnesses reported back to the public on the impartiality of the proceedings." In the period between challenge and duel, intermediaries were often able to arbitrate the dispute without bloodshed. And since these rules applied only to gentlemen, they "made ordinary brawling appear ungentlemenly, vulgar, and immoral." For all these reasons the Davis brothers may have felt the code duello was worth preserving in that lawless society. Their stand was all the more agreeable because it pitted them against their bitter political rivals.[55]

For a decade beginning in the mid-1840s Joseph Davis was very active in the Democratic party. He was a leader in the movement among family and friends to make his younger brother an effective voice in Democratic politics. Without seeking state or local office, except for one unsuccessful eleventh-hour try for the governorship, Jefferson Davis in rapid succession became a congressman, military hero in the Mexican War, senator, and secretary of war. For eight years following the death of his first wife, Jefferson had joined his brother in reading and discussing current affairs while refining their political beliefs. By 1842 they were ready to take an active role in the party of their choice, and both soon appeared as delegates to county and state Democratic conventions. In 1843 Joseph was appointed to the state Democratic committee, and the next year he and Jefferson joined two sons-in-law and numerous friends in forming the Warren County Democratic Association. In 1848 Joseph was a delegate to the national convention in Baltimore, and he remained an active party member through the early 1850s.

Despite joining an established political party, the elder Davis continued to express his independent views. Although he and his brother Jefferson were usually in accord on the various issues, they did not always agree with their fellows. For example, in September 1842 Joseph was chosen as chairman of a convention in Vicksburg called to discuss taxes. One newspaper reported that he "displeased some politicians in denouncing in his inaugural address *all tariffs* as of the same character and effect!" So far from approving tariffs as he had in 1831, by this time Davis, unlike most Mississippi Democrats, did not even accept the use of tariffs to raise revenue. He advocated removal of "all restrictions upon the exchange of commodities with other nations." Always fearing the growth of federal power, he maintained that direct taxation would be "the surest means of preventing extravagant expenditures, and therefore the cheapest mode of supporting the government." Davis believed that a tariff was a very unfair, regressive tax that placed an undue burden on the poor. He argued that the cost of government would be more equitably distributed through free trade and direct excise or property taxes.

Like many of his generation, Davis voiced a distrust of political parties. In 1847 he welcomed rumors that Zachary Taylor might run for president. As Jefferson Davis's former father-in-law, a successful general in the recent Mexican War, a fellow planter, and a close friend of the family, Taylor should have been their ideal candidate even though his party affiliation was unknown. Joseph wrote that he would back him "if he could be the candidate of the nation instead of the party" and if he was "opposed to the Ultra Powers claimed by the whigs for the federal Govt. such as the protective [tariff] and internal improvement policy." A month later, Davis stated that Taylor, "if in truth he is a Southern man . . . may be president and president of the nation not a party." But when Taylor ran as a Whig, the Davises reluctantly supported his Democratic opponent, the northerner Lewis Cass. Although once in office Taylor proved to be no friend of the South, the Davises continued their friendship with him. Jefferson and Varina were at the president's bedside at his untimely death in July 1850.[57]

By 1840 Joseph Davis was keenly aware of sectional differences in the United States, and in his travels he began to defend slavery and southern rights. When he attended a Whig meeting in Lexington, Kentucky, at which Cassius Clay advised Kentuckians to avoid identification with slaveholders of the deep South, Davis became furious and tried unsuccessfully to get the floor for a rebuttal. In 1845 he was concerned because "the last apportionment of members of the house of representatives still further increased the majority of non-slaveholding states in that body, and with equal stride has increased sectional legislation, and the avowal of sectional motives." Davis strongly favored the annexation of Texas but opposed any restriction of slavery in the northern part of it for two reasons: such a distinction would mean "countenancing the idea that [slavery] is an evil only to be tolerated in special cases" and "admitting that the new states thus situated are not upon an equality in the Union" because they were subject to special restrictions. As a child of the Revolution, Joseph Davis had grown up with a profound attachment to the Union. Although he shared his brother's skepticism about some aspects of the Compromise of 1850, at a states-rights convention in Jackson in 1851 he helped draft resolutions rejecting secession as a last resort not justified in the existing circumstances.[58]

There is little doubt that Joseph Davis played an important role as adviser and helper in his brother's early political career. His letters show that in Jefferson's absence in Washington or commanding troops in Mexico Joseph kept in close touch with the maneuvers of Mississippi politicians and intervened on Jefferson's behalf when he deemed it expedient. After the Cassius Clay meeting in Kentucky, he sent his brother a rough statement of events and his opinions on them to edit and send to the press. A few years later, he wrote a letter to a newspaper expressing opinions on current issues that was erroneously attributed to his brother. In his correction, the editor quoted Joseph as saying there was "'nothing in the letter for which [Jefferson Davis] would not be willing to be considered responsible.'" However as the years went by and his national reputation grew, the younger Davis spent less and less time in Mississippi and Joseph became less important as his mentor. The family estrangement in the early 1850s undoubtedly contributed to the weakening of this tie. By 1855, although apparently warm bonds of affection had been restored, Joseph's role was that of an aging father figure always fascinated by his brother's career. On one occasion Joseph was so intrigued with Jefferson's account of affairs in Washington that he declared he would like to "set out immediately for this Island of enchantment." But he realized he could no longer be involved in his successful brother's day-to-day decisions. He was still useful in other ways, however; the Whigs claimed that the Democrats bought a New Orleans newspaper for which "Jo Davis supplied the means" in an attempt "to control public sentiment in Mississippi."[59]

In addition to his activities in the Democratic party, Joseph Davis participated in special conventions called by citizens from time to time to deal with particular problems. In September 1842 he was unanimously chosen chairman of a Planters Convention in Vicksburg held to protest the city of New Orleans's imposition of a tax on cotton shipped to or from that port. Under his leadership the meeting of planters from the plantation counties passed resolutions aimed at withholding their business from New Orleans by using steamships and agents that operated outside its borders. Davis was appointed a director of Vicksburg's Commercial and Rail Road Bank in 1849 and was named a delegate from Warren County to a railroad convention in Livingston, Alabama, the next year. In 1853 he was sent to the Southern Commercial Convention in Memphis, and the next year he was chosen to represent Warren County at the same group's convention in Charleston. Although he did not play a leading role in these meetings, his presence indicates that Davis was recognized as a respected elder statesman who could ably represent his region.[60]

The prosperous master of Hurricane was also noted for his benevolence. He obviously enjoyed helping young relatives, as demonstrated by his gifts of plantations to each of his daughters and to his brother. In addition, he saved the farm on which his widowed sister-in-law was living and provided a home and support for his widowed sister Amanda. He supplied numerous other benefits for young relatives and friends; as a contemporary reported, "Many youths of both sexes are indebted to him for a liberal education." He sent grandchildren, nieces and nephews, wards, and the children of friends to schools in New Orleans and Kentucky. One niece reported, with some exaggeration, that she stayed at Hurricane one year because Davis seemed more cheerful when she was there and she was "the only one of us who has ever had it in her power to show him we at least of the thousands he has benefited do feel thankful."[61]

Some of his gifts implied obligation, however, and required a certain amount of dependency from the recipient. Davis was chronically skeptical of the business ability of family members, in many cases with good reason. This distrust may explain why he seemed reluctant to transmit the titles along with the plantations he bestowed on them. In some cases this caused resentment and legal complications after his death. By withholding the deed to Brierfield for all the years that his brother cultivated the plantation, Davis probably saved the land from permanent confiscation after the Civil War, but he could not have foreseen this advantage during the antebellum period. Both that restriction and the fact that he allowed his daughter Florida only a life estate in Diamond Place probably reflected his persistent fear that unworthy in-laws might somehow gain possession of his beloved property. For him, land continued to hold an almost mystical value as the measure of his true worth and the basis of his security. Fortunately, as his thirty-five-year tenure at Davis Bend drew to a close, he could not foresee the coming debacle that would force him to give up most of his material possessions and find a more basic standard of worth.

FOUR

War-Ravaged Refugee

THE CLOUDS OF WAR WERE GATHERING as Joseph Davis cele-
brated his seventy-sixth birthday on December 10, 1860. A
month earlier, Abraham Lincoln and the dreaded Republican
party had won a victory that boded ill for the maintenance of
southern power in the federal government. Jefferson Davis was
one of the strongest advocates of southern regionalism and a
bitter opponent of the Democratic candidate, Stephen A. Doug-
las. Davis had campaigned for John C. Breckinridge, although
he recognized the danger from party fragmentation. After Lincoln's election, the younger Davis displayed an eleventh-hour
caution and advised the governor of Mississippi against immediate secession. He later claimed that though he never doubted
the right of a state to secede, he was certain that "secession was
the precursor of war between the States," and his experience as
secretary of war had shown him "the total lack of preparation in
the South for war."[1]

At President James Buchanan's request, Senator Davis hurried back to Washington, where he was appointed to Senator

John J. Crittenden's Committee of Thirteen in an unsuccessful effort to effect a compromise. Partly because he knew better than his fellow Mississippians the relative military and economic weakness of the South, and partly because his friendships and experience in Washington gave him a national outlook, Jefferson Davis tried to resist the popular demand at home for an immediate breakup of the Union. Rather than giving the Republicans and the new president additional power by removing southern members of Congress, he urged the disgruntled states to postpone their withdrawal at least until the new Congress had met.

While the younger Davis was in Washington seeking to slow the momentum for secession even as he purchased all available rifles for the mobilizing Mississippi militia, Joseph back at Hurricane heard the widespread rumor that his brother had been mortally wounded in a street fight with Andrew Johnson. Joseph wrote Jefferson that he "disbelieved the report yet felt much anxiety, to know if anything had occurred to justify the rumor." Worry about this false story was only part of a general uneasiness Davis must have felt in early 1861, when Mississippi seceded from the Union on a wave of mass hysteria and his younger brother was forced to resign his Senate seat and return to Brierfield.[2]

Joseph Davis's apprehensions increased in February, when Jefferson was summoned to Montgomery, Alabama, to become provisional president of the new Confederate States of America. Because of Joseph's wide reading and extensive travel, as well as close contact with his experienced younger brother, he shared Jefferson's nationalistic outlook to a great extent. Furthermore, Joseph, who had been born at the close of the American Revolution along with the new United States, knew better than younger men the pain of that birth and the resultant pride and loyalty it inspired. As a lad he heard war tales from his father and neighboring revolutionary war veterans and probably saw the venerated George Washington on his visit to Wilkes County, Georgia. All of these early influences contributed to Joseph's genuine love for the United States, which coexisted with a fierce loyalty to the South. When these sentiments came into conflict, the elder Davis reluctantly accepted their ultimate incompatibility. After the war, he wrote President Andrew Johnson: "My opinion of the right of a state to secede was the same as that of most democrats, that it might be done peaceably, but [I] had been always opposed to a dissolution of the union from the belief that it would destroy the *grandure* and *power* of the *Great Republic.*" In April 1861 he must have been dismayed to learn of the outbreak of hostilities at Fort Sumter.[3]

Life at Hurricane continued to be dictated by the rhythm of the agricultural seasons rather than by the politics of civil war. As warm weather approached, Eliza Davis ordered from their New Orleans merchants a quantity of fine cotton fabric, hoop skirts, crinoline, and silk braid from which the seamstresses could fashion stylish dresses for the women of the household; the family was planning the usual summer escape to more healthful climes. In 1861 Joseph Davis decided that Virginia would be an appropriate destination. His daughter Caroline Leonard lived in Norfolk, where her husband was a newspaper editor, and his beloved younger brother was trying to organize a new government at the Confederate capital, which had just been moved to Richmond. Jefferson's invitation proved irresistible when he added, "Your advice to me[,] always desirable[,] is now more than at any previous period coveted." Furthermore, the Confederate president believed a battle was impending and wanted to go to the front lines himself, leaving his family under Joseph's care. Remote as such action seemed from Hurricane, the elder Davis could not ignore his brother's appeal.[4]

The party that boarded a boat for Memphis in June included, in addition to Joseph and Eliza Davis, grandchildren Joseph, age twenty-two, and Lise, age nineteen; their father, Dr. Mitchell;

97

and two young cousins, as well as several servants. After a brief stay in Memphis they started for Richmond by train, probably because of the federal blockade of Confederate ports. The train trip proved to be an arduous experience involving many delays, but for Lise and her cousin Mary the time passed happily after they were joined by General Richard Taylor, son of family friend Zachary Taylor, and two bachelor officers. At last, the travel-worn group reached the Spotswood Hotel in Richmond, where the Jefferson Davis family and other ranking Confederate officials were staying while awaiting permanent housing. The fashionable hotel, built around a courtyard, was completely occupied, but by nightfall Varina Davis had prevailed upon the management to make room for the Joseph Davis party.

Among the guests at the Spotswood were a nephew of Joseph and Jefferson, Joseph R. Davis, who was the president's aide; a niece, Helen Davis Keary, whose husband was a captain stationed nearby; and numerous friends and acquaintances. In her diary Mary Boykin Chesnut of South Carolina described in detail the social scene at the hotel; she claimed that the women spent their time visiting, gossiping, and flirting with the men, who were vying for places of importance in the new government. It seemed that every man, and especially his wife, thought he could fill a prominent positoin better than the latest appointee, and all were more than willing to second-guess and criticize those with the power of appointment.[5]

On July 21, when the Joseph Davis party arrived in Richmond, the Battle of Manassas began such a short distance away that the guns could be heard at the Spotswood. There was great concern in the city, where many had friends and relatives at the front. According to Lise Mitchell, "There were nine ladies at the hotel whose husbands were in the battle, and the poor half distracted things were constantly coming to my Aunt's [Varina Davis's] room to know if she had received dispatches from the battlefield." Many interested spectators from both Richmond and Washington rode out to see how the contest progressed and succeeded in getting in the way of both armies.[6]

Jefferson Davis went in person into the battle zone, accompanied only by his aide, Colonel Joseph R. Davis. Although he was reckless to risk his life in this way, the president was at heart a soldier who craved military action. He would rather have been a top Confederate general than chief executive; both he and his wife believed he was better suited for that post. Fortunately, he remained unscathed in this adventure and saw his Confederate troops rout the Union army after an indecisive battle. The Rebels failed to pursue the retreating Yankees and, according to later critics, missed a chance to take Washington, but Confederate generals claimed that weary troops, lack of supplies, and heavy rain that turned roads to bogs made it imprudent to attack the well-fortified federal capital at that time. In any case, the people of Richmond were overjoyed with the news of a Confederate victory that trickled back to them along with many exaggerated tales of heroism. Soon the idle women at the Spotswood were busy helping to care for the wounded of both sides in makeshift hospitals set up in tobacco warehouses and other available buildings. The grim aspects of war had begun to penetrate Richmond society.[7]

Two weeks later Jefferson Davis and his family moved into the renovated mansion on a hill that was soon called the White House of the Confederacy, and Joseph Davis took his wife and granddaughter to Norfolk. While visiting Caroline Leonard, they were taken to see the impressive fortifications that failed to protect the city from capture a few months later. They went on a dispatch boat to Fortress Monroe under a flag of truce but only got close enough to see the long line of federal tents along the river before a Union boat intercepted them and received the communication from General Benjamin Huger that they carried. For Lise, at least, this was even more exciting than life at the Spotswood Hotel.

A few days later, the three visitors returned to Richmond, where the president insisted that they stay with his family in the mansion. There a brilliant social season was in full swing. The president and his wife entertained informally almost nightly, and in mid-August they gave an elaborate reception for the members of the Confederate Congress. Eliza Davis wrote home about the beautifully decorated table laden with fruit, cake, and a punch that was especially relished by the guests. According to Lise, the young people in the family, including Cousin Mary and Varina's sister Maggie Howell enjoyed these affairs because they could take visiting young women and soldiers to a back room or the veranda, "where we could laugh and talk without annoying the rest of the company."[8]

Although Eliza Davis complained as usual and longed to return home, claiming she did not want to add to Varina's troubles, she admitted that her husband was thriving on the excitement in Richmond because he "likes to see and talk to people." Many besides the youngsters found it a heady society. Mary Chesnut noted in her diary, "We ought to be miserable and anxious, and yet these are pleasant days. Perhaps we are unnaturally exhilarated and excited."[9]

Joseph Davis finally realized that, stimulating as life was in Richmond, there was little he could do to ease the burden of responsibility that was impairing his brother's health. In fact he feared the presence of his extended family only added to the confusion in Jefferson's home, so late in August the Joseph Davis party departed for a leisurely journey overland to Hurricane. On the suggestion of Judge John Perkins, a family friend, they stopped first to visit his wife and daughter at Conyer Springs on the way from Richmond to Bristol in Virginia. Although the judge had said it was "a delightful place, so cool and quiet," Lise Mitchell declared it "the most unattractive place I had ever visited."[10]

The Davises soon moved on to Montgomery White Springs,

where Lise found more agreeable people, although she admitted that "life seemed very monotonous after the activity and excitement of Richmond." Following two weeks of relaxation at the resort, they resumed their homeward journey, stopping for a day in Washington Springs to see Mary Stamps and her three little girls, who were summering in the cool mountains. Although the Davises urged her to return to Mississippi with them, Mary insisted on remaining near her husband, Captain Isaac Stamps, who was still in camp at Manassas. The Davis party reached home to find all hands busy with the fall picking and ginning of a lush cotton crop, even though the northern blockade and the Confederate embargo prevented its immediate export. The year 1861 ended with the usual visits by family and friends, especially young companions of Lise and Joe Mitchell, all of whom hoped and expected that the inconvenience of war would soon end.[11]

Early in 1862, it became apparent that a Confederate victory would not be easily achieved, and, in fact, the war might become much more disruptive. By late February, after Confederate losses in Tennessee, Jefferson Davis wrote his brother warning of possible danger should the enemy get as far down the river as Davis Bend. The Confederate president believed that he was "the object of such special malignity" that his property and that of his family would serve as "an attraction to plunderers," and he advised Joseph to send their crops, cattle, and slaves to some place of safety, "even up the Big Black." By April, however, the elder Davis, isolated on the Bend, was far more concerned about a local threat because there were heavy rains and the rapidly rising river was already seeping through some of the levees. At first, he kept most of the hands planting cotton and cultivating corn, sending a few to herd the cattle to the remaining dry pastures, but by April 20 he had diverted all available laborers to shore up threatened levees on his and his neighbors' plantations. As the waters neared the record high mark set in the flood of 1859, Davis reported, "Our situation is truly bad." He personally supervised the force of 150 slaves working on the Woods's levee and hoped for the rain to stop.[12]

Meanwhile, word reached Hurricane of the Confederate losses at Shiloh, including the death of the capable General Albert Sidney Johnston. Davis blamed the subsequent southern retreat on General P. G. T. Beauregard, who, he said, "may possess courage & as an Engineer skill[,] but he wants character to command respect." The even more worrisome surrender of New Madrid and Island No. 10 on the river prompted Davis to ask his brother, "Are there no men of character that could be placed on the Miss[?]" Now the Union navy could move southward to menace Memphis. Seeking a haven from both floodwaters and possible enemy action, Davis arranged to have some two hundred bales of cotton from Hurricane and Brierfield sent by boat up the Big Black River.[13]

On April 26 residents of Davis Bend were shocked to get word of the fall of New Orleans. The astonished Davis later wrote that he had considered that great port "more capable of defense than any commercial city in the Confederacy & its fall the greatest misfortune." If the South's largest city was so vulnerable, river planters could put little faith in Confederate ability to protect smaller towns above it such as Baton Rouge and Natchez. Davis immediately ordered his family to start packing and made preparations to leave Davis Bend on the first available boat upriver.[14]

On Sunday, April 27, hearing a boat whistle, they gathered at the landing, but it refused to stop for them, indicating that it was engaged in Confederate service. The next steamer, which proved to be the last civilian vessel to leave New Orleans, arrived at sunset and took the Davis party aboard even though it was crowded and lacked adequate supplies as a result of its hasty departure from port. Although they reached Vicksburg during the night, the passengers remained on board until morning. The Davises found further misfortune at the hotel, where Mary Stamps was staying en route to her family's home downriver. As Lise later reported, "She had arrived in Vicksburg with a sick child who had just died. Away from her husband, in a hotel among strangers, who can picture her agony and distress?" One of Davis's nieces, Anna Bradford Miles, who had been visiting at Hurricane, was going home to Bayou Sara so she was able to help Mary and her two remaining children on their sad journey the next day on the steamboat *Quitman*.[15]

Joseph Davis immediately faced the major problems common to refugees. First, he must find some way to house and feed his dependents under the most distressing conditions. Recent Confederate losses on the Mississippi meant that Union gunboats might soon menace Vicksburg from both directions. By late April, when the Davis party landed there, the town was crowded with Confederate troops reassigned from action in Tennessee and northern Mississippi as well as from New Orleans and Baton Rouge, all busy building fortifications and encampments on the bluffs above the river. The wounded from recent engagements were crowding makeshift hospitals and vying for space and food with local residents, many of whom were preparing to flee the city. As Joseph Davis described it, "the state of things in Vburg was confused," so he, like many other civilians, decided to seek refuge in the country. He shepherded his group aboard a train to Clinton in Hinds County just a few miles west of Jackson. His friend and former overseer Owen B. Cox lived on a plantation nearby, which Davis hoped to use as a base while he sought more permanent accommodations. Arriving at the Cox home late at night in a pouring rain, according to Lise, "we received a welcome so warm that it fully compensated for the annoyances of the trip." Neither Cox and his family nor the refugees realized that this visit would last for many months.[16]

With his family temporarily settled, Davis hurried back to Vicksburg to address his second concern, the removal of more property and slaves from the flooded and insecure plantation at Davis Bend. By Wednesday, April 30, he had "succeeded in getting two flatboats[,] the only oars in the place & a small steamer to tow them down." He persuaded Owen Cox and David Van Benthuysen, Eliza's nephew, to supervise the hazardous venture. They were instructed to bring back valuable papers and books from Hurricane and Brierfield as well as all the slaves they could carry.[17]

In the few days that Davis had been gone, customary discipline on the plantations had been undermined. Ben Montgomery reported that the day before Cox and Van Benthuysen arrived with their small flotilla, a Confederate boat had stopped to recruit laborers for work on the Vicksburg fortifications. Most of the slaves hid from the soldiers, but ten from Hurricane and five from Brierfield were taken against their will. No wonder that by the time Cox had loaded the boats with family possessions there were no slaves to be found. As further evidence of the breakdown of controls, as soon as Cox left, the slaves broke into the mansions and removed whatever they wanted. According to Davis, the two white overseers he had left in charge offered no resistance. He told his brother they seemed "rather to encourage than suppress these charades."[18]

The Union fleet under Admiral David Farragut had shelled Vicksburg late in May with little effect; it was evident that a combined army and navy effort would be required to take this heavily fortified citadel so Farragut withdrew most of his ships down the Mississippi, leaving only six gunboats to keep bombarding the city. In the next few weeks, Davis tried repeatedly to bring more slaves from the Bend to join the growing colony in Hinds County. When another agent proved unable to collect a single one, Davis himself ventured downriver in an open boat. Despite the danger from Yankee gunboats or from exposure, which had cost his father his life nearly forty years before, Davis believed that he must try to rescue his slave force. He succeeded in bringing out some, but many others were too sick to be moved. An epidemic of measles had been carried to Brierfield by a lad who caught it while working on the fortifications at Vicksburg. He had managed to steal a canoe and make his way home, where his illness spread through the quarters at the Bend and later among the Davis slaves in Hinds County. For the moment, Davis halted his efforts to move people and concentrated on saving livestock and crops.[19]

As a patriotic Confederate planter, Davis had joined the voluntary embargo on selling the 1861 cotton crop. The flood and the threat of enemy action caught him with a great deal of his and his brother's net worth tied up in bales on Davis Bend. When he fled in April, most of the cotton that had not been sent up the Big Black River was underwater and therefore seemed inaccessible to the enemy. But in early June, on his way back from Hurricane, Davis was horrified to learn that General M. L. Smith, the commander at Vicksburg, had ordered his men to burn all cotton for twenty miles beyond the Big Black, whether or not it was likely to fall into enemy hands. Davis sent an urgent message to his brother asking him to intervene, claiming, "This order is likely to do much harm & to produce much dissatisfaction." Before Jefferson Davis could act, local newspapers that had always opposed the Davises politically began accusing them of preserving property which ordinary citizens were forced to destroy. A couple of weeks later, Joseph reported to Jefferson, "The two hundred bales of cotton I had taken 30 mi. up Big Black has been hunted up and burned . . . & I see by the papers that yours & mine have been burned at home." The newspaper attacks continued despite indignant denials of wrongdoing by both Davis brothers. Of greater significance to Joseph was the loss of some 841 bales of cotton worth thousands of dollars at a time when the prospects for additional income from another crop looked dim.[20]

Soon the family was further dismayed to learn of another

misfortune that made their refugee status suddenly seem more permanent. On June 24 Admiral Farragut's fleet, under stern orders from the White House to take Vicksburg, steamed back up the Mississippi. Along the way, a raiding party landed at Davis Bend and proceeded to wreak havoc on the Davis plantations, which the Yankees later labeled "the cradle of the Confederacy." They took what furnishings they wanted from Hurricane, then smashed the rest and ripped up all the family portraits. Some deposited sets of china and dishes on the lawn and shattered them with bayonets, while others made a bonfire of the valuable books from the library. The raiders plundered Brierfield in a similar fashion, then, as they returned to their boats, set fire to Hurricane mansion. It burned through the night with the flames visible from the Vicksburg bluffs some thirty miles away. General M. L. Smith telegraphed the bad news to President Davis. Later it was learned that only the Hurricane mansion was destroyed, leaving the empty neoclassical library and the vandalized house at Brierfield still standing.[21]

The loss of his home was a devastating blow to the aged Joseph Davis. For thirty years Hurricane mansion had stood as visible proof of his success and status. It was the seat of his patriarchy, the symbol of his power, not only in the family but also in Mississippi society and politics. The land he had begun accumulating in 1818 and which had consumed his entire attention since 1828 had borne sweetest fruit in the elegant, comfortable home where his roots were firmly established. His sense of bereavement at the loss was so great that, although he did a great deal of traveling in subsequent years, Davis could never again bring himself to set foot on Hurricane plantation.

But the old man did not brood over his misfortune. He had always fulfilled his responsibilities as head of the family and master of a large slave force, and he was determined to continue doing so. The most pressing problem he faced in June was providing adequate care for the slaves. He had some seventy of his and more than twenty of his brother's at Cox's place in makeshift accommodations. When possible, he hired them out to work on the fortifications or in the hospitals in Vicksburg, although he noted wryly that everything was very costly except labor. He continued his efforts to transfer more people from Davis Bend to Hinds County, but even when Joe Mitchell or Joe Nicholson succeeded in bringing some upriver, others slipped away from Cox's place and returned to the Bend. Although Davis's model slave community was in disarray, the blacks still felt safest there under the leadership of the resourceful Ben Montgomery.

In early July another Yankee raiding party took several slaves as well as a mule, some harnesses, and a cart from Hurricane, prompting Davis to begin a campaign to persuade Confederate officers to send troops to capture such marauders when they were separated from their boats. General Earl Van Dorn at Vicksburg brushed aside the request, claiming a shortage of men and implying that he was occupied with more important matters. The master of Hurricane continued to press his demand intermittently for the next year; he seemed to feel he could not let the violation of his ideal community go unpunished.

Throughout that rainy summer, Davis continued to worry about the health of his family, his slaves, and his livestock. Poor housing and irregular meals contributed to a high incidence of pneumonia, which combined with the aftereffects of the measles and the usual depredations of malaria to produce widespread illness and numerous deaths. During the three summer months, Dr. E. G. Banks treated from two to seven seriously ill people on each of his eleven visits to the Hinds County community of Davis slaves. Colder weather in the fall only increased the prevalence of respiratory diseases.

The white family experienced poor health, too. Seventeen-year-old Joe Nicholson contracted typhoid fever while on a trip to Davis Bend and remained bedridden there for more than a month. Although the young people were usually indisposed for only brief periods, Eliza, who was a semi-invalid before the war, seemed to fade steadily under the stress of exile from her home. In August Davis took her and Lise to Coopers Well near Jackson, where many refugees from New Orleans and the river plantations sought health and diversion. Eliza wanted her husband to stay with them there, but he maintained that his health was fine and he could not tarry. Instead, he spent most nights at his niece Ellen Anderson's house in Jackson, where he could ride out to check on conditions at Cox's place almost every day.

The horses, mules, and cattle fared as poorly as the humans in those troubled times. Davis first sent some of them to a place south of the Bend near Rocky Springs, but they were not well cared for there so he had Joe Mitchell bring those that were well enough to travel to Hinds County. Davis wanted to take them and the stock he had sent across the Pearl River east of Jackson to some safer place still farther away from the Mississippi, but enemy action in northern Mississippi made him question the safety of that plan, and by the end of the summer he had decided to send the mares and young colts and some of the cattle back to Davis Bend. Conditions were so bad where they were that some had died and others had strayed off. He was convinced that the rest would die of starvation or be confiscated by the army if they were not moved.[22]

As soon as he left Hurricane, Davis began looking for another plantation where he could attempt to recreate as nearly as possible the agricultural self-sufficiency and social community of the Bend. Just days after his original departure, as he chartered boats to bring more valuables up the river, he began searching for an alternative place. As a result of a chance meeting with Rankin Dirkson in Vicksburg, Davis agreed to lease a large plantation owned by Dirkson's wife's family. Dirkson claimed that the place had good land for cultivation, extensive pasturelands, and "ample buildings ready for occupation." After arranging for Cox to load his stock, slaves, and possessions on the train, Davis went ahead to arrange for receiving them. At the new place he was shocked to find the land and buildings completely inundated by floodwater; he rushed back to Jackson just in time to intercept his freight and return it to Cox's place. By now it was mid-May, and after losing two weeks Davis found that "every place for rent had been overflown."[23]

It seemed apparent that the only way to secure a plantation was to buy one so Joseph Davis enlisted the aid of his friends to that end. Unfortunately, he found that the price of land had increased with the demand. One place with rather mediocre soil but with enough housing to accommodate all the slaves was offered for $40,000, which Davis considered exorbitant. He told his brother, "This might be sold again for the purchase money but such a debt I am unwilling to incur." Other available places had inadequate buildings, and he soon discovered that it would be impractical to plan extensive construction because of the high cost of materials. He needed a place that could provide food as well as shelter for his and his brother's bondsmen.[24]

Owen Cox, whose hospitality the Davis party was undoubtedly taxing, proved to be an indefatigable helper, traveling for a week at a time searching for a plantation and also for leather to make shoes for the hands. Meanwhile, Davis hesitated to accept his nephew Hugh Davis's offer to care for Jefferson's slaves on his plantation downriver. Joseph was reluctant to relinquish his authority and to separate a community that had been cohesive before the war; instead, he sought to buy two adjacent plantations for his brother and himself. As he explained in October, "I wish to get them near together for although I can effect but little its better for the negroes to have some one that they can look to for protection."[25]

The search and the uncertainty placed an increasing strain on the elderly planter, who became more desperate for a solution as the fall wore on. Although he claimed that he still had "some hopes that the war may end soon," he realized that he "must act as if it [would] last for a series of years." Continuing his search, he would think he had found a place only to discover that it lacked enough corn in the fields or crib to tide them over till another crop could be grown or adequate housing to keep out the winter rain and cold. By the first of November, to solve what he termed "a cause of much anxiety," he announced his decision "to remove to Texas or the north Eastern part of La." But before he could implement this decision, he was struck down by a serious illness that confined him to bed at Cox's house for nearly three weeks. During his incapacity, further enemy advances led him to abandon the idea of leaving the state, but he continued to worry about his problem. When he was finally offered an adequate plantation in Hinds County by a planter who visited him in his sickroom, he agreed to buy it sight unseen.[26]

Dr. Thomas J. Catchings owned a medium-sized plantation called Fleetwood near Bolton's Depot, some fourteen miles west of Clinton and about halfway between Jackson and Vicksburg. Recent Yankee successes led him to expect further fighting along that corridor so he decided to move his family to their other plantation in Washington County. When he heard of Davis's quest for a place, Catchings saw a chance to sell at a good price property that he believed to be at risk of imminent destruction, so he hurried over to Cox's, where he found the old man ill and depressed. Catchings described his plantation in glowing terms as including a large, two-story house with four fireplaces, all six rooms ceiled, plastered, and weatherboarded, with venetian blinds at the windows. Connected to it was a frame addition of six more rooms with four fireplaces. There were two smokehouses and two servants' rooms in the backyard as well as thirteen slave cabins, which were of prime importance to Davis. Catchings claimed that his place was well supplied with water, including "two never-failing wells curbed with stone, one large brick cistern, & plantation ponds always with an ample supply of water." Of equal concern to Davis, the owner stated that he would also leave on the place some one hundred hogs large enough to butcher, about the same number of sheep, and three thousand bushels of corn, as well as about six hundred bushels of sweet potatoes and twenty stacks of fodder. This supply of food for slaves and stock was vital to Davis because he had learned that almost nothing had been produced at Hurricane and Brierfield that year.[27]

This sounded like the answer to Davis's vexing problem so, when Catchings agreed to include the furnishings in the house, Davis offered to pay $10,000 for the 1,306 acres of land and another $10,000 for the personal proprety, half to be paid immediately with a note for the balance payable in January 1864. He instructed Cox to give Catchings $2,000 from Davis's purse and promised to have the remainder of the down payment in his hands within two weeks in exchange for the deed, which Catchings agreed to prepare. Both men seemed satisfied with the contract, and Davis immediately began to recover his health.

The very next day, with Catching's permission, Davis sent a group of his slaves to the new plantation and arranged for Ben Montgomery to send up others along with some stock from Hurricane. A few days later, Edward L. Miles, Davis's nephew by marriage, and Cox made the trip to Fleetwood with some of the Davis property and an additional $5,000 of the down payment. To their surprise, Catchings refused to accept the money because it was not the entire sum he expected. The next morning, as Cox and Miles were leaving for home, Catchings announced that he had decided to rescind the contract. He tried to return the $2,000 he had received from Davis, claiming it would be inconvenient for him and against the wishes of his wife to move. In fact, the real, though unstated, cause of the problem was Catchings's reluctance to accept either the down payment or the promissory note in Confederate currency, which was depreciating with every Yankee victory. By the end of 1862 inflation had progressed to the point that it took seven Confederate dollars to buy what one dollar had bought two years earlier. Dr. Catchings, however, did not want to seem unpatriotic by voicing his qualms to the president's brother. Cox later testified that Catchings told him "if Mr. Davis gets the place he will have to get it by law."[28]

Cox refused to accept the returned currency, and he and Miles hurried back to tell Davis of the complication. Immediate action was required because the entire first payment was due the next day. On Davis's instructions, Cox and Miles rode to Clinton, where they borrowed the required amount from a merchant who knew Joseph Davis. When Cox then returned to Fleetwood to offer the owner the entire down payment, Catchings again refused to accept it. When informed of this, a deeply disturbed Joseph Davis left his sickbed and rode into Jackson to consult his old friend Judge William Yerger. The judge said that Catchings could not be forced by law to accept a note payable in Confederate money. Instead, they drew up a note promising to pay $10,000 without specifying in what currency. James T. Rucks, a member of Yerger's law firm, took that note and the rest of the down payment in Confederate money out to Fleetwood, where he persuaded Catchings to accept it and give him the deed. Catchings later testified that he regarded Davis as "one of the mighty men in the land, as he really was from his wealth, talents, & high connexions," therefore Catchings wanted to avoid a quarrel with him, "well knowing that in a controversy with such a person, so connected, [Catchings] would be under a disadvantage." Whether by intimidation or not, Joseph Davis at last could end his seven-month search and try to rebuild his harmonious community on a new plantation of his own.[29]

The Davis family and their baggage arrived at Fleetwood the night of November 26, 1862, and Joseph was shocked by the conditions he found. The next day in a letter to his brother he called it "a poor place with miserable huts for a part only of the negroes." He later described it as an inferior plantation "without a sufficiency of water for either persons or stock, & very little timber, either for firewood or rails,—no stables, or barns, & the negroe cabins not capable of sheltering the inmates from the rains; the dwelling house of logs, & very little furniture; instead of . . . 3,000 bushels of corn there was less than . . . 1,000 bushels on the place; not more than twenty-five or thirty hogs, instead, as represented, one hundred, that were to be fattened for pork for the next year, & only a few sheep."[30]

Other members of the Davis family seemed more resigned to the fact that their new home was far inferior to Hurricane. Eliza was still in such poor health that she welcomed any place where she could settle down, although she was not strong enough to assume her usual role as manager of the household. Dr. Catchings later claimed that soon after their arrival Eliza had told him of her "entire satisfaction with the comfort & convenience of the house & said she intended to keep it for her place of residence." Obviously not sharing her husband's resentment of the former owners, she graciously consented when Mrs. Catchings requested some pieces of furniture from the house which had sentimental value for her. Lise, too, was tired of being a guest and happy to have a home of their own, where she quickly assumed the duties formerly borne by her ailing grandmother. She later complained of the strange hodgepodge of a garden planted by the former owners and was horrified that they had let the chickens roost in the yard, but she seemed cheerfully determined to make the best of it.[31]

For the next six months the family enjoyed a life that seemed almost as serene as during the antebellum days at Hurricane. Lise was delighted to be able to entertain visitors even in their makeshift accommodations. Young ladies and their gentlemen friends came out from Jackson or Vicksburg and often were joined by soldiers on furlough for a house party at Fleetwood. Just before Christmas, Anna Bradford Miles arrived from Kentucky after a harrowing journey through enemy lines disguised as a nun. She remained at Fleetwood for months to be near her husband, who was serving with Confederate troops in Mississippi. To the delight of the Davis family, Lise's brother, Joseph Mitchell, arrived soon after Christmas on leave from General John C. Breckinridge's staff in Tennessee. Joseph Davis was grateful for the assistance of his grandson in his efforts to collect slaves and livestock and rebuild an efficient plantation.

Late December also brought a visit from the president of the Confederacy, who was dissatisfied with the performance of his generals in the West. Joseph Davis, who never hesitated to express his opinion, had told his brother, "The generals allotted to us have been a miserable lot," and Jefferson was inclined to agree. After General Earl Van Dorn lost one-quarter of his army in an unsuccessful attempt to retake Corinth, Jefferson Davis replaced him with General John C. Pemberton as commander in charge of the defense of Vicksburg. (Joseph Davis was pleased, candidly commenting that "when Van Dorn was made a General it spoiled a good Captain.") The president also appointed General Joseph E. Johnston commander of all Confederate troops between the Alleghenies and the Mississippi, hoping he could coordinate the army of Braxton Bragg in Tennessee with that of Pemberton in Vicksburg. At the request of Mississippi Governor John J. Pettus as well as to quiet his own doubts, Jefferson decided to tour the western battle fronts. He hoped his presence would both buoy morale and stiffen defense efforts. Arriving in Vicksburg on December 19, he and Johnston reviewed the troops and inspected the defenses for two days, then traveled by train through Jackson to Grenada to see Pemberton's army. On December 26 the younger Davis addressed the legislature at Jackson, where Johnston then set up temporary headquarters while the president went on to Fleetwood for a brief visit.

His worried family was grateful for the opportunity to see the careworn Jefferson, whose heavy responsibilities were jeopardizing his health. On this visit he was in good spirits, having received word of Van Dorn's successful cavalry raid on Holly Springs. This foray destroyed Grant's essential supplies and, along with Nathan B. Forrest's destruction of his supply lines to the North, crippled the planned Yankee overland advance into Mississippi.[32]

Early in 1863 Joseph Davis completed arrangements on behalf of his brother to buy a fifteen-hundred-acre plantation just three miles west of Fleetwood. It was a prosperous place but cost some $33,000, including the hogs, corn, and fodder. Joseph paid the owner the required $5,000 down payment partly from funds Jefferson had sent him and the rest from his own savings. He hired an overseer of doubtful worth and immediately made arrangements to bring the rest of the slaves from Brierfield and Hurricane to Hinds County, although he recognized that only those who were willing to leave would come. He sent Thornton Montgomery with instructions to Ben to prepare both people and equipment to board the boat he had hired from Porterfield. It was clear that Davis still considered Montgomery his most reliable assistant on the Bend. The transfer was successfully completed, but Davis was outraged when he received a bill for $1,200 for the use of the little steamboat. He reported, "I thought the claim unreasonable & declined to pay it."[33]

His dwindling money supply was a source of serious concern to Davis. The concentration of Confederate troops in the area to protect Vicksburg and Jackson put added pressure on the food supply and sent prices soaring. Davis was able to sell some mules to the quartermaster but faced heavy competition for needed supplies. Salt was especially scarce and almost prohibitively costly. Confederate taxes caused another drain on Davis's financial resources. To pay the state war tax for himself and his brother he had to buy a special issue of scrip, which, he reported, had been "bought up by the speculators," who were selling it for twice its face value. This tax amounted to more than $1,500 for the Davises. With little prospect of producing more than enough to provide bare subsistence that year, he was worried about how he could pay next year's taxes. It had been many years since this successful planter had faced the specter of financial want. Still, as spring flowers bloomed peacefully in the garden, Eliza's health seemed to improve, and Joseph Davis knew some satisfaction as he contemplated the twenty new houses finished for the slaves.[34]

This comparative serenity was threatened late in April by the news that General Ulysses S. Grant had given up the futile canal and bayou operations that had occupied his troops since February. Successfully moving ships and men down the river past Confederate batteries at Vicksburg, the Yankees landed in force below Grand Gulf and soon took Port Gibson. By May 7, as they marched northeast toward Jackson, Davis reported that his neighbors were leaving and urged him to do the same, but he said, "I am less frightened or less able to move so shall remain." On May 12 the Yankees took Raymond, not far south of Bolton Station, then moved on to the east. General Johnston's forces were driven out of Jackson two days later. After sacking and burning much of the capital, Grant turned his army toward Vicksburg, and Bolton lay right in their path. The day after the Fleetwood occupants heard of the fall of Jackson, a Confederate soldier came dashing in to warn them that federal troops were within a mile of them. Just then a blue-coated cavalry unit came in sight, and the Rebel horseman cleared a high fence and was gone.[35]

In this first encounter with Yankee soldiers, the Davises fared well. When the commanding officer demanded to talk to Joseph Davis, both his wife and granddaughter insisted on accompanying him onto the veranda because they feared he would be taken prisoner. Although the officer asked many questions which Davis answered with dignity, no attempt was made to harm them or their property. Lise believed the Yankee was afraid to enter the house; he mumbled something about waiting for his column to come up and then rode away. Fortunately, the main body of the army did not pass along that road, although they soon sent a squad that, according to Davis, "carried off most of the negroes, stock of horses, mules, oxen, wagons, carriages, and other property." In protest Davis sent a letter by the offending Yankee officer addressed to General John A. McClernand, a Democratic politician from Illinois and the only Union officer he knew personally. The letter requested the general's protection for "a 'non combatant' in my 79th year," whose family consisted of himself and "four ladies, three of whom [are] invalids." He never received a reply.[36]

The next night, after all the family except Davis and Lise had retired, they heard a noise outside and found the house surrounded by mounted men. After some insolent remarks, the officer in charge sent a detail to search the house for firearms, taking all their guns, including Lise's two little shotguns. The next day, as more Union cavalry passed, many stopped to take whatever they wanted from the storeroom or the yard, but again they left the house unmolested. One group called Davis onto the porch hoping to engage him in a political argument. He prudently declined to reply, but, as Lise noted, she and Martha Harris, who was now a member of the household, "gave free expression to a few of our sentiments."[37]

On May 16 the bloody Battle of Champion Hill was fought within earshot, just a few miles from Fleetwood, causing the Davises great anxiety. When the smoke cleared, the Union army had won at the terrible cost of 2,440 men killed, wounded, or missing, while the Confederates had lost a proportionately more devastating 3,840 men. The next day some Yankee soldiers came to Fleetwood and, according to Davis, "entered, and passed through, every part of the house, not sparing the sick rooms, broke open the store rooms and carried off the provisions and family supplies." That night another group came in and broke open desks and trunks searching for valuables. By now the family was distraught, and when Davis got word that a squad would arrive the next day to burn the house, he insisted that Lise and Anna Miles take the remaining carriage and seek shelter with the Andersons in Jackson, which Union troops had evacuated. Eliza Davis and Martha Harris were not well enough to make such a journey so they remained with Davis. Also present was a visitor from Vicksburg, Dr. Morris Emanuel, who was president of the Southern Railroad.[38]

As expected, a Union party commanded by a Lieutenant Miller arrived with orders from General Peter J. Osterhaus to burn the house. Miller gave Davis half an hour to remove the furniture. As Davis and Emanuel, aided by the few remaining slaves, carried out the furniture and deposited it on the lawn, the Yankees broke open previously hidden trunks and took whatever silver and jewels had escaped earlier detection. The invalid women were carried out in time to watch this looting. Both Davis and Emanuel remonstrated with Lieutenant Miller, and Davis again scribbled a futile note of protest to General McClernand.

The soldiers had just lighted the torch to destroy the house when the slaves shouted that Captain Joseph Mitchell had arrived. When the Yankees saw the Confederate in uniform enter the house from the rear, they assumed he had a company with him and they fled, burning the corn house and other outbuildings on their way. In fact, Joe had come alone to check on the welfare of the family. Although the Fleetwood house was saved for the moment, Davis reported that "such was the shock that the sick had received that it became necessary to remove them farther into the interior." The next day a prostrate and enfeebled Eliza Davis and ailing Martha Harris went to stay with the Cox family near Clinton. Hearing that her grandfather was alone, Lise left Anna Miles in Jackson and returned to Fleetwood, where she and Davis remained undisturbed for nearly a month while Grant's forces besieged Pemberton's army at Vicksburg.[39]

Feeling fortunate to have a roof over their heads when most plantation houses had been burned, including the one on Jefferson Davis's place nearby, Davis and Lise moved the bedraggled furniture back indoors with the assistance of the few remaining slaves. Then they all cheerfully returned to as normal a routine as possible. With vegetables and fruit from their garden and chickens that the enemy had overlooked, Lise and the cook were able to set a fine table. They sent surplus food to General Breckinridge's nearby camp, where both Joe Mitchell and Joe Nicholson were stationed. One evening at Mitchell's request Davis and Lise gave a very successful dinner party for the general and his staff, who lingered for several hours. They talked optimistically of the impending Confederate victory after General Johnston got reinforcements and marched to the relief of Vicksburg. Lise was so encouraged by their confidence that she reported sleeping well for the next few nights, "always, however, with a revolver under my pillow."[40]

Joseph Davis was not so sanguine about their future prospects. Fleetwood was in the no-man's-land between Confederate forces at Jackson and the Union troops that ringed Vicksburg. Davis deplored the army's failure to assign soldiers to keep order in their area, leaving the remaining planters and their slaves at the mercy of marauding bands of Yankees or stragglers. By mid-June many of his and most of his brother's slaves had left their plantations. When Union soldiers marched on after camping on Jefferson's place for two days, the blacks refused to go with them, but a few nights later most of them mysteriously disappeared. Davis believed that "the promises made them were more than they could resist" and they realized that the country was "in the power of the enemy," whose "orders must be obeyed." Before adding those who stayed at his brother's place, Davis reported that his remaining work force consisted of "eight men mostly old and some women & children." At first, he set the able-bodied blacks to work rounding up the remaining cattle and mending fences, but by mid-June, as his hopes of victory dimmed, he directed them to repair old carts and wagons the Yankees had not considered worth confiscating. Several weeks earlier his brother had urged him to bring his family to live in the presidential mansion in Richmond, but Joseph had declined to leave his Mississippi responsibilities. Now, as further flight seemed inevitable, Joseph reluctantly sought possible means of transportation.[41]

All the Confederates were becoming desperate as Grant tightened the noose around Vicksburg and General Johnston failed to send reinforcements to Pemberton's aid. Stories filtered out about the hardships endured by the seventeen thousand soldiers and perhaps five thousand civilians inside the city. The Davises had heard earlier that Julia Porterfield and her family were living there in a tent, but under the constant Union bombardment from land- and river-based cannon they, like most civilians, probably sought shelter in newly dug caves. In the heat of the summer, as food grew ever scarcer, the sick as well as those with war wounds filled makeshift hospitals amid the rubble and the stench of rotting horses. No wonder the morale of the besieged gradually declined as weeks went by without relief.

Confederates outside Vicksburg felt the desperation too, and now, for the first time, Joseph Davis undertook to influence his brother's military decisions. Colonel E. J. Harvie, a member of General Johnston's staff, became distressed at what he saw as political posturing at the expense of the Confederacy. He therefore wrote to the elder Davis without the general's knowledge asking his intervention to get the president to order General Bragg's troops to reinforce Johnston and save Vicksburg. It seemed that, although he was empowered to do so, Johnston was hesitating to act because he was unsure of the political repercussions. Harvie insisted that only President Davis could make the decision to move Bragg from Tennessee because it might leave that state vulnerable. But Harvie and Joseph Davis both felt that saving Vicksburg, and with it the entire Mississippi Valley, was crucial and therefore worth the political risk. The elder Davis had been consulting with Johnston's staff regularly, and when they convinced him it was necessary, he agreed to contact his brother. On June 14, before receiving Harvie's petition, he had sent a telegram to Richmond saying it seemed that Johnston "intends to surrender the Country to the enemy[.] Cannot some remedy be speedily applied[?]" On June 22 he wired his brother, "Can the army of Genl Bragg be sent to the relief of Vicksburg[?] The safety of the Confederacy is involved."[42]

He emphasized this message in letters he wrote almost daily giving his appraisal of their generals: Pemberton "has industry[,] zeal & courage but wants order. . . . Judgment . . . & . . . the important quality of inspiring his men"; Johnston "is a dull man" who also lacked the ability to inspire his soldiers. As a result, Davis noted an increasing feeling of discouragement among the men that might prevent them from exerting the maximum effort necessary to overcome the enemy's superior numbers. Already he detected among the Confederates an alarming trend toward "straggling and desertion." Without absolving the generals of blame, the frustrated Davis asserted, "I think the spiritless condition of the country is mainly due to the *Press,* the *Preachers* & the *crokers* & if the country is lost we may justly charge them with it."[43]

By June 24, when he had received no answer from his brother, Davis sent a final desperate wire: "Is it possible to reinforce Johnst[on] or must Vicksburg fall[?] Pls reply to this[.]" Although the old man apparently did not receive it immediately, President Davis shot back an agonized reply: "Reinforcement to the extent now asked is impossible without ruin to the Confederacy. I have spared no effort and am still striving to give aid to the defenders of my home, but that is not my only duty. I mourn over opportunities lost and if I may will endeavor to rep[air] the injury." The beleaguered president had repeatedly expressed his deep distress at the sad plight of his elder brother. Jefferson found it especially frustrating "to feel powerless to give [Joseph] the personal assistance which in the order of nature is due from me." But with a major Confederate offensive in progress in Pennsylvania and their forces in Tennessee threatened, he felt unable to send more troops to aid in the defense of Vicksburg.[44]

About this time General Johnston, although still refusing to commit his unreinforced troops, began tentatively moving toward Grant's army to see if he might cautiously assist the embattled Pemberton in evacuating Vicksburg. The sick and starving men inside were in no condition to initiate a daring escape. On July 3 Pemberton asked Grant for terms of surrender, and on July 4 the siege of Vicksburg officially ended in complete Confederate defeat.

Having sent a message warning Davis of the impending surrender, General Johnston arrived at Fleetwood early in the morning of July 4 to brief Joseph Davis on the situation and urge him to flee. Lise Mitchell and the servants served breakfast to the general and his staff while members of their retreating army straggled past. Then, after lending their host "one of the public wagons, team and teamster" and urging him to leave without delay, the officers rode off to resume their commands.[45]

Davis and Lise immediately stowed beds and bedding, pots and pans, and a few cherished belongings in the wagon, climbed into their remaining carriage pulled by some old mules, and rode away from Fleetwood. They were followed by those slaves who chose to join them, traveling in crudely mended ox-drawn wagons piled high with their clothes, bedding, and a few housekeeping necessities. Enduring the heat of the July sun and the dust of the retreating army, they finally reached Clinton, where they were joined by Eliza Davis and Martha Harris with her little daughter Margaret. Leaving his plantation in the care of a friend who had sought refuge there, O. B. Cox hastily loaded up his family and belongings to accompany the Davis caravan. They soon caught up with and passed through the Confederate army retreating toward Jackson. The Davis party found the capital in a panic, momentarily expecting a Yankee attack, so they hurried through town and had just crossed the Pearl River when they heard the first shots.

Thus began the harshest phase of Joseph Davis's refugee life. The group traveled all day at the snail's pace of their ox-drawn wagons along dusty or muddy roads, camping at night near an abandoned cabin if possible where the older people could seek shelter. The others slept in tents made from carpets stretched over poles. At Enterprise in eastern Mississippi they encountered a Confederate encampment whose kind commander gave them an army tent. They were forced to rely on farmers along the way to sell them the food they cooked over their campfires.

Davis felt responsible for the entire entourage, black and white, but his major concern was the deteriorating health of his wife, Eliza. Whenever possible he secured a bed for her in a local farmhouse, but the poor food, uncomfortable accommodations, and uncertainty about the future caused her condition to worsen day by day. Even though camping in the dampness must have aggravated his rheumatism, Davis sustained the appearance of good health and good spirits in order to maintain group morale and confidence in his leadership. More than once this trek must have brought recollections of his family's difficult journey from Georgia to Kentucky when he was a child more than seventy years before. Despite all the years of living in comfort and ease, the hardihood and skills acquired during his pioneering boyhood once again stood him in good stead.

After traveling eastward for three weeks, the group found

themselves in Choctaw County, Alabama, near the Tombigbee River, a safe distance from General William T. Sherman's army, which had turned back toward Vicksburg. All were exhausted and the stock could go no further so they established camp in a pasture beside a small stream. Most of the party slept in a deserted three-room cabin without fireplaces, but Davis managed to find lodging for himself and his wife in a nearby farmhouse. There they remained for nearly a month so that people and animals could rest and recover. Although the farm family was very kind and did their best to assist her, Eliza continued to grow weaker. Now she was often in severe pain, much to the distress of her husband and granddaughter, who attended her constantly.[46]

Davis was also worried about his dwindling financial resources, so he sent Cox to investigate the possibility of hiring out the able-bodied slaves to the saltworks. Late in August, when that scheme proved impractical and Eliza's health did not improve, Davis decided to move the company to Lauderdale Springs in eastern Mississippi, where a friend, Dr. R. N. Anderson, was a surgeon at the Confederate hospital. He hoped the climate would be better for the invalid and the slaves could be employed as nurses at the army facility.

After an uncomfortable journey, the elder Davises and Lise enjoyed the Andersons' hospitality while the rest of the group were housed in an old, dilapidated house. By scouring the neighborhood and surrounding farms they managed to accumulate enough old furniture and household equipment, and in a few days a fairly comfortable room was ready to receive the weak and weary Eliza. It was fortunate that she had this quiet refuge because she grew steadily weaker and more emaciated. On September 28 Davis reported that she was confined to bed but "free from pain or nearly so." Six days later, attended by the Episcopal bishop, she died quietly and was buried temporarily in a vault in Lauderdale Springs. Joseph Davis was grief-stricken. Despite her years of ill health, his devotion had never faltered since his marriage to the sixteen-year-old Eliza some thirty-six years before. Although relieved that death had brought an end to her suffering, Davis felt that this bereavement added to a crushing burden of woes he must endure. Now he clung more than ever to his attentive and beloved granddaughter, Lise Mitchell.[47]

It was fortunate that the old man had so many people dependent on him that he could not afford to abandon himself to grief. He simply had to provide for "his people" in those chaotic times. While still in Choctaw County, Alabama, he had sent O. B. Cox and young Joe Nicholson back to Fleetwood to see if they could recover any of their abandoned possessions, but they reported that the house and its contents had been burned. The silver and other valuables that the family had carefully buried had been discovered and removed, and the books from their library were scattered about. At Cox's place the Yankees were guided by a former slave to the loft of a log outbuilding. There they found hidden boxes of books and private papers belonging to both Jefferson and Joseph Davis, broke them open, and either took them as souvenirs or tore and trampled them underfoot. The soldiers also found and drank the large cache of fine wines Joseph Davis had carefully stashed nearby. The caretaker at Cox's place was able to save the cherished bust of Jefferson's deceased son, little Samuel Davis, by claiming it was his child, but few other things remained. Even though he knew chances of recovering much were slim, Davis determined to go back himself in the hope of finding some of his livestock or crops to carry with them to a more permanent place of refuge.[48]

Another reason for Joseph Davis to make the long trip back to Hinds County was his wish to bring out more of the slaves from Hurricane and Brierfield. He was motivated partly by the desire to preserve more of his valuable property; if he ever expected to establish another successful plantation he would have to have laborers. But he also felt a genuine concern for the wel-

fare of his people and feared they would be exploited if left un-
protected. As his brother had written a few months earlier,
"The faithful deserve to be saved from the fate to which the
Yankees would consign them." Joseph had sent Jim Green, one
of his most trusted servants, to learn the fate of those left at
Davis Bend. Green had reported that Ben Montgomery and
family had been "carried off" by the Yankees when he failed to
produce a large sum of money they insisted his master had left
with him. Davis did not entirely accept that story, although he
learned much later that the Montgomerys had voluntarily moved
to Ohio under the patronage of a federal officer. Davis noted, "I
have little confidence in any of them."[49]

The master of Hurricane was outraged when he heard rumors about the violence caused by a Confederate cavalry raid
on Hurricane and Brierfield a few months earlier. On his way
back to Hinds County, he stopped at the Confederate encampment in Meridian, where he found and talked with nine slaves
who had been captured on Hurricane and Brierfield. From their
account and official reports he received subsequently in Jackson,
he learned that a Confederate cavalry detachment under a Lieutenant Harvey went to Davis Bend, where they were startled to
meet a band of armed blacks. The Yankees, who had been raising the gunboat *Indianola* from the river opposite Hurricane,
had hired the slaves to cut wood and herd cattle for them. They
had given them some guns to protect the cattle and slaughter it
on demand. The Rebels were so shocked to see armed blacks
that they asked no questions but opened fire, killing a total
of ten of the slaves. They rounded up about fifteen more and
hanged a retarded lad as an example to other potential arms-
bearing blacks. They then beat a hasty retreat, claiming they
were fired on by a gunboat and saw a group of sixty marines
advancing on them.

Davis discovered that there was no gunboat and only one

lone Union marine, who was some distance away arranging to buy more wood. The men the Confederates captured and took to Meridian were ragged and barefoot and told their master they had not threatened anyone. Davis was furious at this slaughter of innocent people and told his brother that "such atrocities should not go unpunished." But there was little he could do except insist that Joe Mitchell accompany any future raid on Davis Bend. That fall, at least two more unsuccessful attempts were made to recover the Davis slaves. In each case the detachment got only as far as the Big Black River but was afraid to cross because of rumors of large Yankee forces on the other side. Although they were directed to continue on to the Mississippi and burn the gunboat *Indianola,* these men complained that their real mission was to recover Jeff Davis's slaves, and they were unwilling to take risks for his enrichment. One major infuriated Joseph by spreading the false rumor that "Jeff Davis and his Brother had been selling cotton to the Yankees." In spite of these reluctant agents, Davis lingered in the Jackson area hoping Joe Mitchell would be able to accompany a successful foray to the Bend.[50]

Lise Mitchell, who accompanied her grandfather on this journey, described the sad sight that greeted them as they drove the familiar road from Jackson west to Clinton and on to Bolton and Fleetwood: "Where only a few months before were comfortable dwellings there remained only groups of chimneys standing amid ashes." Davis's hopes of finding anything of value were disappointed. All the horses and mules and any usable furniture had disappeared. He reported to his brother that "the hogs had been stolen by the people of the neighborhood at both places & the stock turned in and the crop destroyed[.] All the tools and implements carried off." He found a few books and papers that were worth packing up to store with some of the friends with whom they visited. Lise was pleasantly surprised to find at Cox's place that "one of the house servants had managed to save a few books of mine, among them the set of Audubon's 'Birds and Beasts of North America.'"[51]

Finally, after lingering in Hinds County for nearly three months and gathering only a few willing blacks, Davis decided to take Lise and return to Lauderdale Springs. He knew that it was important to get settled on some land in time for spring planting if he were going to feed his entire party for another year. The question was where to find a secure location. The Coxes made other arrangements. After much preparation the Davis group, including about forty slaves, set out traveling eastward, but they encountered so many delays and breakdowns with the old wagons that they soon learned that Union troops were only a few days' march behind them. Moving with all possible haste, they managed to cross the Tombigbee River safely. There Davis left them to camp while he went to seek advice from General Leonidas Polk, who was camped a short distance away. Polk suggested that they head for southern Georgia. Davis later wrote his brother, "I made some advance in that direction but after the retreat of Sherman & finding the difficulty of reaching there I stop[p]ed." Davis then decided to turn northward to the much closer town of Tuscaloosa, Alabama.[52]

Dr. Anderson, who had recently been transferred from Lauderdale Springs to the Confederate army hospital there, had sent a message urging the Davises to join him. The Anderson family had not yet gotten possession of a house they had agreed to rent and were temporarily crowded into three rooms of an office building. Setting the blacks to work planting corn on a plot of land across the Black Warrior River, Davis made plans to house his family with the Andersons in their new place "as a joint stock concern," sharing expenses as well as a house. For the time being, though, the Davises sought temporary accommodations.

They were warmly received by the townspeople. Davis and

Lise were invited to be the guests of Colonel Robert Jemison, a former Confederate senator and one of the most prominent men in that part of Alabama. Davis liked Jemison, whom he described as "a man of remarkable energy[,] industry and Judgement with a large & widely extended interest." Their lively discussions of the many political and military issues of common concern were especially beneficial to the elderly Davis, who had been completely preoccupied with grief and worry for several months. Lise was equally pleased to visit the Jemisons because she enjoyed their daughter Cherokee, with whom she "formed a deep and lasting friendship." Their mansion was the largest of the gracious homes on tree-lined Greensboro Street and became the wartime center for many social activities in this pleasant town. Lise and her grandfather stayed with the Jemisons throughout April and most of May. When young Joe Nicholson was sent back from his unit because he was seriously ill, Mrs. Jemison generously insisted on taking him in as well.[53]

At last, late in the spring, the rental farmhouse some two miles out of town was ready for occupancy. The large Anderson family included several young children in addition to Lucy, who was Lise's age, and a grown son, who soon left for the army. Davis gladly joined them, bringing Lise, Martha Harris and her daughter Margaret. Joe Mitchell and Joe Nicholson were frequently there on leave, making a household that rivaled in size the one at Hurricane before the war. Friends and neighbors in Tuscaloosa lent spare pieces of furniture and equipment so that the two families were able to keep house in comparative comfort.

For nearly a year life went on routinely in Tuscaloosa. Prices of food and other necessities kept increasing so Davis set the slaves to work making shoes and spinning and weaving cloth as well as raising corn and cutting and selling wood. These measures slowed the drain on his dwindling cash reserves. Dr. Anderson, who received a regular salary from the government, paid all the household expenses, but Davis kept a careful account of his debt for these expenses, which he promised to repay after the war.

In the spring of 1864 the Confederate division stationed in Tuscaloosa was visited by a number of high-ranking officers, and Davis as usual hastened to give his brother a candid appraisal of each man. He believed that some of them were "more concerned for ease & safety than the country's service," and they met in Tuscaloosa because "it is a pleasant place." Concerned about their apparent reluctance to fight, he concluded that "they should be employed, for if they are left idle they will be cut[t]ing each others throats."[54]

While Lise kept busy planning and participating in such charitable events as the tableaux, in which she represented a sultana in one scene and Night in another, Davis found a new friend for himself. The exiled *Mississippian,* now being printed in Selma, held a short story contest which was won by Elizabeth Avery Meriwether, a young Confederate wife trying to support her three sons in Tuscaloosa. Davis was impressed with her story, called "The Refugee," based on her difficult life since General Sherman had driven her out of Memphis for her outspoken defense of the Rebel cause. Admiring her articulateness and literary skill, Davis located her and introduced himself. Their acquaintance soon blossomed into friendship, and he spent many pleasant hours sitting on her porch, where she said later they discussed "everything under the sun, from myths of the ancient Greeks to the latest ailment of my Baby Lee." Meriwether spent most of her time and energy providing food for her young children with little help from her husband, who was an officer at the front, so she welcomed a stimulating social interlude. At first sight she expected the elderly Davis to be tedious like most old people, but she found "my visitor proved anything but tiresome." He had lived a long time, "seen much of the world and he knew how to relate his adventures in an entertaining way." Joseph Davis missed his wife and craved the company of an intelligent woman. Meriwether claimed that Davis offered to marry her should her husband be killed. Perhaps he made this suggestion facetiously in response to her worry about her children's future. In any case, their friendly relationship brightened the days of exile for both of them.[55]

Concern for his brother and for the future of the Confederacy was never far from Davis's thoughts as 1864 drew to a close. General John B. Hood's disastrous Tennessee campaign and the loss of Savannah at Christmas time brought gloom to the refugees in Tuscaloosa. By early 1865 the interior of the Carolinas and most of Alabama were the only untouched Confederate areas, and Grant determined to overrun them. He sent thirteen thousand men from Tennessee into Alabama to destroy the munitions complex at Selma and then seize Montgomery, while another Union division invaded southern Alabama through Mobile. When these operations began in March, Davis was still primarily concerned for his beleaguered brother, who was suffering "badgering by congress" and many of his fellow countrymen. But Davis remained hopeful of improvement in their fortunes, concluding, "I am still looking for good news every mail."[56]

In April the war came to Tuscaloosa with the approach of Union troops. When wild rumors seemed to be credible, Davis took Lise in their trusty carriage with the same old mules driven by their faithful servant Jack and braved the muddy roads into the country. The first time they left home they happened to stop at the farm of a very helpful family who gave them sanctuary for a few days until the danger passed. The next alarm sent them back to the same house. The third enemy raid came from another direction, however, so they were forced to take a different route and found no such refuge. The Yankees stole the poor little mules and some of Davis's clothes from his trunk in spite of Lise's vehement protests in the face of drawn guns. The mules were later found abandoned and returned to Davis. By April 19 they knew that Selma, Mobile, and Montgomery had fallen, but these seemed minor losses compared with the occupation of Richmond. When news of Lee's surrender reached them, there was no longer room for hope, and everyone seemed to sink into despair.

Davis was uncertain what to do next and seemed slow to pick up the pieces of his shattered life. His responsibilities had diminished somewhat; with unusual initiative, Martha Harris had taken her daughter to Kentucky to attend school and be near her son in St. Louis. Davis was thus relieved of responsibility for their support. The Davis blacks were being harassed by roving bands of ruffians, however, and their old master had to drive out to their defense late one night. He faced down the intruders that time but worried about a recurrence. He told the former slaves that he expected them to support themselves, but they remained dependent on him for assistance.

In mid-May the Anderson family departed, leaving Davis and Lise to manage the Tuscaloosa house alone. Lise found the arrangement "much more agreeable than living with so large a family." After their paroles the two Joes joined the household, and Lise enjoyed cooking for the group. Their major worry concerned the fate of Jefferson Davis, whose capture on May 10 they did not learn about until June. In July both Lise and her grandfather became ill and spent two months slowly recovering. Depression because of their defeat and uncertainty about their future took a toll.[57]

Finally, Davis decided that he must return to Mississippi. In early July he had sworn a loyalty oath officially witnessed by a captain of Minnesota volunteers, but he realized that this piece of paper would not guarantee the return of Hurricane and Brierfield. In late September he wrote a letter to President Andrew Johnson describing in detail his tribulations during the war and asking that his property be restored. Without waiting for an answer, he and Lise packed their few belongings and, accompanied by some forty homesick former slaves, headed homeward. According to Lise, "Grandpa and I traveled in the carriage drawn by the same little mules we had used for the greater part of the war, Jack retaining his place as driver." She continued, "Having lost nearly all we took with us from home we were not troubled to bring much back."[58]

Nearing his eighty-first birthday and nearly penniless, Joseph Davis had endured the rigors of life as a refugee with remarkable resilience. Undoubtedly his pioneer childhood, requiring adjustments to frequent moves and unexpected crises, had prepared him well for these trials late in life. On the long journey home he must have reflected on the vagaries of fortune that had left him in such a sad condition. But he knew that now he must somehow summon the strength and determination to build a new life for himself and those dependent upon him.

FIVE

Peace at Last

THE JOY OF THEIR RETURN TO MISSISSIPPI in early October 1865 was dimmed for Joseph Davis and his granddaughter Lise Mitchell by the condition of the countryside through which they traveled. From Meridian to Vicksburg they were awed by the destruction left in the path of Sherman's 1864 expedition. In the towns through which they passed lonely chimneys were all that remained of most businesses and many residences, while similar sentinels marked the sites of former plantation houses along the road. Lawlessness and civil strife had run rampant across Mississippi since the surrender in May. To quell it, the provisional governor, William Sharkey, had called up the local militia despite opposition from the U.S. Army commander. In justifying his action to General Osterhaus, the governor noted that "twelve of fifteen consecutive nights, passengers traveling in the stages between here [Jackson] and Vicksburg have been robbed . . . within twelve or fifteen miles of your own headquarters." Only their lack of worldly possessions protected the Davis party from such attack.[1]

While the blacks in their entourage eagerly pushed on to Hurricane and Brierfield, Davis and Lise paused for a few days with friends and relatives in Jackson, where postwar lethargy was slowly yielding to a brief flurry of reconstruction. But Davis was anxious to get back to the Mississippi River so they soon drove on to Vicksburg.[2]

By the fall of 1865 this city had patched up most of the damage caused by bombardment during the siege of 1863 and was bustling with new life. Although about one-quarter of all white males above the age of fifteen in Mississippi had died from battle or disease, the towns were full of disabled veterans seeking employment. Since they were physically unable to work on farms and plantations, many tried to make a living in merchandising or clerical jobs. Hundreds of northerners, many of them former soldiers, also settled in Vicksburg and invested their capital, hoping to make a fortune from the cotton business. Northern wholesalers set up agencies there seeking to replace New Orleans factors by dealing directly with merchants and planters along the rivers and the newly restored railroad routes. Vicksburg was also headquarters for the military district, and in coming months several regiments of federal troops, both black and white, were mustered out there with money to spend. In addition, freed slaves had been congregating in the town since before the federal occupation and now occupied a teeming area of shacks and burrows on the hillside. Between 1860 and 1870 Vicksburg tripled both its population and its gross sales of merchandise; it was indeed a boom town.[3]

After only a few days there Davis drove on to Diamond Place, where his daughter Florida had managed to weather the war. Here he faced the true extent of his problems; Diamond Place was a typical example of the damage done to fields and levees by enemy action and four years of neglect. Although he had received some news before leaving Alabama, he now heard directly from Ben Montgomery details of the much greater destruction at Hurricane and Brierfield, just a few miles farther downriver. He also realized that the major repairs necessary to restore his place would require the cooperation of a large and willing labor force, something that was in short supply since emancipation. As he matched his needs and those of his dependents with his physical capacity, Davis decided that he could not resume personal direction of his estates. He did not even have the heart to visit Hurricane and see for himself the ruin of all that he had built during his lifetime. So without complaining or explaining to his family, he took Lise back to settle in Vicksburg.

As in most war-torn urban areas, housing was scarce. Joseph Davis was not financially able to live in a hotel, but he found comfortable accommodations by relying on family connections; he and Lise settled into a boardinghouse operated by Florida's foster daughter Julia Porterfield and her husband.

William Porterfield, an Irish immigrant, had settled in Vicksburg in the 1830s. In the antebellum decades he prospered, combining the steamboat and insurance business with his interest in wharf property. After the death of his first wife, he married Julia Lyons, some twenty-four years his junior, who bore him five sons.

In 1851 the Porterfields built Shamrock, an elegant mansion on Mulberry at Oak Street, high above the river. The three-story brick house was divided by long, spacious halls, with four bedrooms on each of the upper floors. On the first floor there were two large parlors paneled in hand-carved walnut. Across the hall was the grand dining room, measuring some twenty-four by forty-two feet with a floor of blue and white marble, two fireplaces of carved white marble, and seven tall windows commanding views of the landscaped grounds and the river beyond. The house had suffered remarkably little damage from the Yankee bombardment. One shell entered the door on the river side, passed down the hall, dislodging a bit of plaster, went out the front door, splitting off part of one Corinthian column, then tore off the top of a cedar tree in the yard. Porterfield, who was too old for combat, zealously defended Shamrock; on one occasion he killed a Confederate soldier and wounded two others who were caught prowling on the grounds.

This site of festive prewar parties now provided a gracious setting for feeding and housing numerous paying guests. William Porterfield died of apoplexy in November, just a month after the Davis party arrived, but Julia continued operating the boardinghouse as a means of supporting her young boys. Here, with a minimum of effort, Joseph Davis found a refuge from which he could attempt to recapture some of his former prosperity. Sitting at a writing desk in his room watching the traffic on the river, he began the struggle to regain his property. Shamrock was not his home—Hurricane was gone forever—but it was a comfortable place run by kinfolk in a familiar city where he could easily contact those whose aid he required to accomplish his mission. The mansion proved a welcome haven to the weary refugees.[4]

For the next eighteen months Joseph Davis was completely engaged in an effort to restore the viability and productivity of his plantations at Davis Bend. During the last year and a half the Yankees had undertaken to build there a model colony for refugee slaves, including a large hospital and the Home Farm for dependents. Most of Hurricane had been divided into small plots that the army leased to freedmen organized in a self-governing community. The abolition-minded officers who directed this effort claimed to have effected miraculous development of the former slaves, never realizing that the colony was in many ways merely carrying on the antebellum tradition of self-government experienced by the Davis slaves.

Benjamin Montgomery and his family had returned from their wartime home in Cincinnati to resume leadership of the enlarged black community at Davis Bend. In the summer of 1865 the Montgomerys organized a group of black leaders to seek to lease the cotton gin at Hurricane from the federal government. Although Ben had been chief engineer and manager of that vital operation throughout the antebellum years and certainly knew more about it than the inept carpetbagger who had held the lease the previous year, the Yankee officer in charge of the Freedmen's Bureau in Mississippi refused to grant him and his group the lease. Enraged by this rebuff and other abuses perpetrated by the Yankees at Davis Bend, Montgomery poured out his grievances to a receptive Joseph Davis even before his return to Vicksburg. Both Montgomery and Davis shared a common goal of restoring Hurricane and Brierfield to productivity as quickly as possible so they had no trouble resuming their prewar cooperation even though their attitudes toward the Yankee victory clearly differed.[5]

As soon as word reached Davis Bend that "Marse Joe" had returned to the area, a procession of former slaves came to visit him with tales of injustice that they blamed on the Freedmen's Bureau. The Montgomerys brought him copies of their correspondence with the authorities regarding the gin lease and recounted their unsatisfactory experience with unscrupulous agents the previous year. Others added to the list abuses they had suffered under northern management even before the Montgomerys' return. They claimed that when the Yankees occupied the Bend in December 1863 they confiscated many of the blacks' horses, mules, and oxen as well as carts and other equipment, making it difficult or impossible for them to cultivate a crop of any kind. As hordes of refugees were brought to the Bend, some of the Davis slaves were forced out of their homes and suffered from exposure. The indignant blacks asserted that the Yankees even tore down the large, modern water cure hospital, hauling away the furniture and machinery. These violations of the comfort and welfare of "his people" infuriated Davis at least as much as the confiscation of his property. In his mind, their cause and his own were united, and the Freedmen's Bureau became the main obstacle to their resumption of a productive life on the plantation. All the frustration and disappointment of the painful refugee years now fueled Davis's passionate struggle with this hated symbol of northern victory.[6]

The brunt of Joseph Davis's attack on the Freedmen's Bureau was borne by the young assistant commissioner for Mississippi, Colonel Samuel Thomas, who during that fall of 1865 was himself struggling to regulate black-white relations under radically changed conditions. On October 9 Davis had just arrived in Vicksburg and was still accumulating charges against the bureau when he chanced to encounter Colonel Thomas on the street. Hoping that his letter to President Johnson from Tuscaloosa would bring the return of Hurricane and Brierfield, Davis asked Thomas on what grounds the bureau held his land. Thomas replied that he had conquered Davis Bend after three days of hard fighting, which Davis disputed since there were no Confederate troops for miles around at that time. When Davis asked for names of the officers involved in the supposed battle, Thomas said he did not remember and impatiently ended the conversation.

Davis returned to his rooms and scribbled a rough draft of a letter describing his interview with Thomas and listing the freedmen's grievances. He then dispatched an "informed machinist," John T. Donaly, to Hurricane to inspect the cotton gin and report on its condition and the extent of repairs made by the new white lessee. On October 21, when he received Donaly's certified report, which was very critical of the Yankee gin operation, Davis sent it to Thomas with the letter enumerating alleged abuses at Hurricane and Briersfield. He made a detailed list of the costs of ginning a bale of cotton, showing that the bureau agent's charges were excessive and claiming that many blacks were being forced to sell their cotton in the seed at great loss. Davis's letter was a respectful request for redress because "surely such injustice, practiced upon the ignorant and helpless should not be tolerated."[7]

On the same day, Davis signed an agreement with Ben Montgomery for the cultivation of as much Hurricane land as he could manage in 1866, paying Davis one-third of his crop. Since Davis was not in possession of the land he was leasing, the document had little value, but he and Montgomery hoped that by sending it to the bureau for approval they might speed the process of restoration. It was the time of year when plans must be made if there was to be a crop in 1866, and both men were financially dependent upon that income.

On October 25, impatient for a reply to his letter, Davis walked down to Colonel Thomas's office on Harrison Street near Cherry. He inquired if his letter had been received, and when Thomas acknowledged that it had, he asked when he might expect a reply. The annoyed Thomas merely snapped "Soon!" and ended the interview. Angered by this abrupt treatment, Davis hurried home to take up his pen and seek redress from higher authority. After writing several drafts in the next few days, he poured out all his grievances in a letter to General O. O. Howard, commissioner of the Freedmen's Bureau in Washington. Before mailing this appeal, he wrote again to Thomas, relaying the complaints of two more of his former slaves who had made the trip up to Vicksburg to seek his help in reclaiming their property held by the bureau. When this second letter brought no response two days later, he resumed his rambling petition to Howard in a more vituperative vein. Stating that "the wrongs committed by authority here must be unknown to you, and . . . if known would receive condemnation," Davis listed them, and then harshly attacked Colonel Thomas as a liar who probably expected to profit personally from cotton grown at Davis Bend.[8]

That same day Davis wrote another letter to President Johnson with two purposes: first, to thank him for restoring his property because Davis had "seen in various newspapers that you had done so." Davis was soon to learn that those rumors were false. But his major purpose was to alert the president to "the greatest evil under which the country now labors," the Freedmen's Bureau, which was "demoralizing the negroes, robbing & defrauding them of what little they possess, and the fruits of their toils." Davis attacked Colonel Thomas by name, although using less harsh language than he had to General Howard. By telling the president that he had reported the situation to Howard for correction, Davis hoped to add executive pressure to his plea.[9]

There was good reason for the elderly Mississippian to expect Andrew Johnson to support his attack on the bureau. The president had been receiving similar complaints from prominent leaders whose advice he heeded. Two months earlier, William L. Sharkey, whom Johnson appointed provisional governor of the state, had warned him that the bureau was "badly mismanaged here" and doing much harm. About the same time, the president referred a letter he had received to O. O. Howard, noting, "The within is but one of many earnest remonstrances daily received at this office against the further toleration of the gross abuses committed under the pretended sanction of law & the authority of the Govenment by its corrupt agents. There will be a thorough investigation, & all such abuses corrected as far as possible."[10]

Such admonitions were always sent on to the local offices so Colonel Thomas had already found it necessary to respond to Davis's first appeal to the president. By coincidence, on the same day that Davis wrote to Howard and Johnson, Thomas issued an order creating a special board of inquiry "for the purpose of hearing & adjusting the complaints & claims of Joseph E.

Davis . . . & such other parties as may have complaints of abuse, detention of property, or dishonesty on the part of officers or citizens on Davis Bend." The three men appointed to the board, a chaplain and two lieutenants, were all officers of Negro troops under Thomas's command. As Ben Montgomery reported to Davis ten days later when the board held hearings on the Bend, "they proved to be nothing more than members of the same clan and may approve of the acts of those here."[11]

When the board moved its hearings to Vicksburg in mid-November, Joseph Davis retained four respected lawyers to represent the freedmen and himself. His chief counsel was Judge D. O. Merwin, who had been briefly imprisoned in July for challenging Yankee authority by issuing a writ of habeas corpus for the release of a planter held for trial by military authorities. William B. Sloan, a Democratic lawyer in Vicksburg for almost thirty years, and Walker Brooks, an antebellum Whig leader and former U.S. senator, also joined the Davis team. Assisted by the octogenarian, they prepared lists of grievances and statements of witnesses. In an effort to strengthen his case by including a lawyer with pro-Union credentials, Davis asked the assistance of Armistead Burwell. No friend of the Davises, Burwell had opposed secession and willingly cooperated with federal occupation after the fall of Vicksburg. In 1859 he had bought the mansion called the Castle built by Davis's son-in-law, the late Thomas E. Robins. During the siege of the city, the house was destroyed and the impoverished Burwell was now struggling to recover his fortunes and his practice among hostile former Confederates.[12]

Davis visited Burwell's office to request his assistance, carefully explaining that neither he nor the freedmen could pay any fees immediately. When the lawyer agreed to consider their plea, Davis gave him copies of all relevant correspondence. That afternoon the two men went to the office of the Freedmen's Bureau, where they observed the board of investigation in session. Burwell later asserted that he was dismayed to find no freedmen present, although he had been led to believe that he was to represent them. He also noted that Judge Merwin was ably presenting Davis's case. At the time, Burwell made no comment, but that night on Freedmen's Bureau stationery he wrote a short note to Davis stating, "I do not think that I can be useful to you or to the negroes in the proposed investigation and decline any further attendance on the case."[13]

Furious at what he considered gross neglect of duty, Joseph Davis fired back an accusation: "The obligations of counsel and client are the most sacred in social life. After a long experience, you are the first that I have known, after possessing himself of the facts and circumstances at the hour of trial has desserted his trust." Exercising some restraint, Davis omitted a sentence included in the first draft of the letter: "I hope your remorse may be less than that of Judas Iscariot."[14]

This accusation of unethical behavior from an arch-Confederate was more than Burwell could bear in silence. He spent the next five days drafting a vituperative reply that covered two closely printed pages, which he then circulated. The rambling argument claimed that Davis was no friend of the freed slaves but was "merely using their names for your own seditious purposes, to make petty war of litigation and strife, against an odious Department of an odious Government, which you have done all in your power to destroy." After accusing Davis of the basest sort of treason, Burwell said that he would ignore Davis's misstatement if he had not been subject to similar malicious attacks since the Rebel surrender. He suggested to the authorities that "instead of temporizing and arguing with traitors, I would urge the most prompt and effective measures of force to quell and exterminate them." These intemperate sentiments expressing the frustration of an unpopular loyalist pleased Colonel Thomas in the Vicksburg bureau; he sent Burwell's printed statement to his superiors in Washington.[15]

The investigating board continued to meet and hear witnesses. According to notes taken by the Davis side, Colonel Thomas was called to give sworn testimony on two occasions. He explained the circumstances of the takeover of Davis Bend, excusing the confiscation of houses, animals, and farm equipment as army policy. Nine freedmen were called to testify regarding their grievances, among them Ben Montgomery, whose questioning was directed by Colonel Thomas behind the scenes. Joseph Davis was annoyed and drew up a formal complaint to the board because he was forbidden to question witnesses and hence prevented from developing his case. He also protested the time consumed by the board's president, James A. Hawley, "in lecturing and insulting witnesses." This quasi-legal military proceeding provided an opportunity for the officious Yankee chaplain verbally to chastise his erstwhile enemy, a leading Confederate, and Joseph Davis did not accept his punishment patiently.[16]

When the board finally submitted its fourteen-page report, Montgomery's original assumption that the judges would approve of the action of their fellow bureau officers proved correct. They explained away the complaints of the freedmen one by one, suggesting that all they needed was more information. In the case of a black man who had rescued a colt from the flood only to have it confiscated, the report recommended the animal's return if it could be determined that ownership would not revert to Joseph Davis.

The board reported that the true source of trouble was Benjamin Montgomery, whom they termed "a man of great shrewdness & intelligence & considerable education." They concluded, "It is apparent that most of the disturbances with Mr. Davis & with the Negroes spring from him." They attributed his discontent to disappointment at not getting the gin lease and deplored his lack of gratitude to the government when he was prospering in both his planting and retail operations.[17]

Ben had been concerned about the evident hostility of the bureau toward himself and his family since Davis had begun pressing their complaints. A short time earlier, Colonel Thomas had threatened to imprison the black leader for making a contract with Davis, a person disloyal to the United States. Nothing came of this threat, but Montgomery became increasingly apprehensive about the consequences of incurring bureau hostility and sought to discourage the strident protests of his former master. On the night of November 18, while in Vicksburg to testify before the board, Montgomery wrote a careful letter to Davis saying that when he originally laid the facts before him he had not realized how disturbing the struggle would be. He suggested that they now soften their attack. Montgomery continued, "I am unwilling to press our complaints too far, which might prove a great loss and much inconvenience to you and yours, without any benefit to us more than be considered, more restless and dissatisfied than others of our color and condition."[18]

Joseph Davis was unwilling to be muzzled, however, and he continued to harass the Yankee officers as much as possible. In its report the board found "the conduct of Mr. J. E. Davis . . . exceedingly incomprehensible and unbecoming." It reported "his language often so severe and ungentlemanly as to require that he should be rebuked and silenced." As a result of his behavior, his counsel eventually abandoned his cause, according to the board. It concluded that his action "was evidently intended as a covert assault on the Government we represent." So Davis had succeeded only in alienating all the bureau officers as well as Armistead Burwell and, to a lesser extent, his other lawyers without greatly improving the lot of "his people" or recovering his property. Although his intemperate outbursts may have helped relieve his unbearable frustration, they were clearly counterproductive for the achievement of his primary goals.[19]

As the end of the year approached, neither Samuel Thomas nor Joseph Davis showed any signs of reconciling their conflict.

General O. O. Howard had made a whirlwind trip through the South, including a very brief stop in Vicksburg, but both Thomas and Davis missed him. Thomas, who was called to another part of the state, said he deeply regretted missing a chance to seek Howard's advice because "it is so difficult for me to tell the course I should pursue." He was in a quandary concerning how much control he should return to local officials while still protecting the freedmen. Davis, who had hoped to put his much smaller problem before the general in person, said that Howard's stay was so brief that "he had left town before I heard of his arrival here."[20]

Having abandoned hope of redress of his grievances by the local Freedmen's Bureau, Davis returned to his letter-writing campaign. On November 25 he composed a fourth letter to President Johnson in which he summarized previous complaints and stressed the urgency of early restoration of his property for the sake of the freedmen. He reiterated that he had given no aid to the rebellion and would complete whatever formality was necessary to restore his estate. The next day Davis sent this with a cover letter to W. L. Sharkey, former provisional governor, who had been elected to the United States Senate and would soon be going to Washington hoping to take his seat. Davis sought the senator's assistance because he knew that Sharkey was on good terms with the president.[21]

One obstacle to the speedy return of the Davis land was cited by Samuel Thomas in the long letter to his superior, O. O. Howard, which accompanied the report of the board of investigation. After defending all the actions he had taken at Davis Bend since its occupation two years earlier as in the best interests of the freedmen, Thomas turned his attention to "Mr. Davis," whose letters he had failed to answer because they were "incoherent, querulous & full of misstatements, & therefore beneath my notice." Thomas asserted that the old man was using fictitious complaints by the blacks as a means to get his property back. Furthermore, according to Thomas, Davis "refused to take the oath of allegiance before the board, & declared that he would never ask for a pardon." Therefore, Thomas believed he had no right to the land, and the bureau would lease it to freedmen again next year.[22]

Since Joseph Davis had sworn an oath of allegiance before a federal officer the previous July while still in Tuscaloosa, it seems evident that he did not object to doing so. Perhaps he refused to repeat the oath before the board because he was annoyed with them and doubted their authority. In any case, he had always refused to ask for a pardon because he felt that he had done nothing wrong. He told all his correspondents that he had taken absolutely no part in the war and had remained quietly at home until driven out by military action. A month later, Charles J. Mitchell, his former son-in-law and Lise's father, wrote that he was surprised to learn that Davis had refused to apply for a pardon: "I was disappointed that you should make yourself perhaps the only example of a large property holder not to submit to the condition imposed upon all alike." He believed that "the example would be thrown away upon the Southern people, whilst the Yankee command's would rejoice in your ruin & the hope of plunder." Mitchell concluded that Davis must have reasons of his own for his refusal, but those reasons still remain obscure. Perhaps his stubborn stand merely reflected his general disgust with postwar conditions; certainly he made evident his contempt for federal authority as embodied in the local Freedmen's Bureau personnel. Thomas ended his letter to Howard by reporting that Davis had called at his office that day and acknowledged that he was the author of the vituperative letter to the commissioner in Washington. Thomas concluded, "I ordered him out of my office, & cannot take any further notice of him or of letters that he may send me."[23]

Davis was not deterred by the open break with Colonel Thomas. Instead, he again sought support from higher authority in his battle against the local bureau. Two days after his hostile interview at the bureau office, he repeated his charges against its agents in a detailed appeal to the Radical Republican senator from Massachusetts Henry Wilson. Quoting from a speech in which the senator had deplored atrocities currently being committed against the freedmen, Davis proposed to present his case as supporting evidence. He summarized the alleged abuses of Davis Bend blacks and his ineffectual petitions to the same Freedmen's Bureau officers who would reap the cotton profits from the plantations. Emphasizing the demoralization of the workers, he asserted, "Formerly a negro did not expect a white man would cheat him or tell him a lie, now he expects nothing else." Explaining his own involvement, Davis said that he had reared most of the blacks on the place with "parental tenderness," and they "have always looked to me as their protector and friend." He continued, "I may claim to have spent more time and money than any abolitionist in the endeavor to improve their condition and elevate their character," and therefore he found it painful to see them "subjected to such cruelty and injustice." To demonstrate his benevolent attitude, Davis added, "For the last twenty years I would gladly have set them free if I had seen any way for their security in their altered condition." This may have sounded self-serving to a skeptical Republican senator, but Joseph Davis was undoubtedly sincere in his protestations. He had been a kind and generous master who was concerned about the welfare of his slaves and deplored the entire system. From the first, he regarded his bondsmen not as chattels but as people with the same feelings and capabilities as whites. But Senator Wilson must have found that hard to accept. For corroboration, Davis referred him to "Hon. Wm. L. Sharkey who is now I believe in Washington." In closing, he recalled that he had met the senator at West Point in 1860.[24]

It is interesting to follow the course of this petition through the government bureaucracy. On January 3 Senator Wilson sent it to the Executive Mansion, where it was rerouted to Commissioner O. O. Howard at the Freedmen's Bureau. Howard sent it on to Colonel Thomas in Vicksburg, as he had Davis's other letters. When the return report from Mississippi reached Howard, he wrote Davis a critical letter because "you accuse Col. Thomas of Murder, Corruption, and prostitution of his office for personal gain." Howard asserted that such a respected officer must be heard in his own defense so he had referred the matter to "the Dept. Commander" for investigation. In March, Major General T. J. Wood sent his report back to the Freedmen's Bureau, and on April 27, 1866, the entire file was returned to Senator Wilson. In spite of Davis's protesting reply to Howard's letter, which was not included, the papers received by the senator exonerated the actions of the bureau officers at Davis Bend. Nevertheless, these and similar charges lodged by Davis and others embarrassed the bureaucracy of the Freedmen's Bureau in Washington, who came to regard Thomas as a liability. In May he was removed from Mississippi and reassigned to the Washington office. For a number of reasons he was not replaced; the military commander in the state also assumed the duties of assistant commissioner of the Freedmen's Bureau. Since General Wood was very responsive to white planters, Joseph Davis might have felt that this phase of his struggle had been successful.[25]

In fact, however, Davis had laid his case before the general several months earlier and had succeeded in antagonizing him just as he had Colonel Thomas. Even before O. O. Howard, prompted by the letter to Senator Wilson, requested General Wood to conduct an investigation of his charges, Joseph Davis had sent Wood papers documenting the alleged abuses of the freedmen. After a cursory review and perhaps a conversation with Thomas, Wood returned the papers to Davis with strongly critical remarks claiming that he was not entitled to any consideration until he had been pardoned. An infuriated Davis scrawled several drafts of a reply to General Wood, who, he claimed, obviously had not read the evidence presented. Davis especially resented Wood's terming the appeal he had sent to Howard "a very disrespectful in fact *insolent* letter." The old man asserted, "We must have fallen upon evil times when to report to the officer having the power to redress grievances, the wrongs suffered by his subordinates, and the dishonorable conduct of his officers is deemed *insolent.*" Davis concluded that Wood's reply must have been dictated by Colonel Thomas. Once again Davis had alienated local Yankee authorities, and although he detailed this fracas in a new letter to the president, which he probably never sent, he was increasingly discouraged. In a letter to Dr. Mitchell in Texas, Davis, not usually given to self-pity, wrote in reference to the evil times that had befallen Mississippi, "and few I think have been more unfortunate than myself." He deplored the fact that "everything here is under military Controll and the insolence of them is insufferable."[26]

Rather than yielding to despair, Davis decided to tap a hitherto unused resource—his prominent national acquaintances. As a lifelong Democrat and frequent participant in national conventions, he had made many friends who might be moved to assist him in his dire need. Senator-elect Sharkey had taken Davis's petition to the president, who referred him to General Howard, but the commissioner of the Freedmen's Bureau had managed to block return of the plantations. Now Davis decided to go farther afield with his appeals. In late January, spurred by Ben Montgomery's concern about securing labor contracts for the new year, Davis prepared a brief summary of the proposed contract and expressed his fear that the freedmen would become vagrant and scattered. He enclosed this statement with a covering letter to Senator James Guthrie of Kentucky reiterating his inaction during the war, his troubles with the Freedmen's Bureau, his current poverty, and the need to recover his property. Davis made an open bid for Guthrie's pity, asserting, "I write with difficulty being now in my 82d year, with loss of strength[,] loss of hearing, and imperfect sight." He hinted that he was singled out for exclusion from his lands because of his relationship with Jefferson Davis. Guthrie apparently forwarded this letter to the Land Division of the Freedmen's Bureau, where it was duly filed without action.[27]

Davis did not abandon his appeals to the president. Upon reading Johnson's message vetoing the proposed extension of the Freedmen's Bureau bill, Davis drafted but did not send a long congratulatory letter reiterating his own grievances against the bureau. With uncharacteristic tact, instead of sending this letter, he coauthored with W. T. Sawyer a brief and highly laudatory message thanking the president for his "able, Statesmanlike, and patriotic" action, which "will place you high on the list of Patriots and Statesmen." Davis expressed the same approval in a brief speech in Vicksburg a few nights later at a mass meeting of citizens who endorsed the president's action "in vetoing the accursed measure." Although realizing it would not help matters, the old man took full advantage of this opportunity to air his grievances against the bureau before a wildly approving audience of fellow southerners.[28]

Continuing his campaign to win influential support, Joseph Davis detailed his plight to his sister-in-law Varina Davis when she and her baby stopped to visit him in Vicksburg in late March. Traveling with her was Burton N. Harrison, former private secretary to Jefferson Davis. Joseph requested his assistance, and Harrison immediately wrote a letter to former Confederate General Richard Taylor, who was in Washington on a mission to the embattled president. Outlining the quest for recovery of Hurricane, Harrison noted that the previous fall "all the newspapers contained a statement that the president had ordered the place to be restored." Believing that "subordinates have interfered to obstruct its consummation," Davis could see no other reason for the delay in implementing the order. Harrison asked, "Can you not bring the attention of the President to the matter?"[29]

When there were no results a month later, Davis finally yielded to the advice of relatives and friends and officially asked for a pardon in an oath witnessed and certified by Judge D. O. Merwin of the criminal court of Warren County. Instead of sending the oath to the president himself, he decided to seek the backing of as many prominent men as he could muster. First, his friend N. B. Moulton added a letter asserting that he knew Davis well, "sitting with him for several hours each day, reading to him from the papers" and discussing public affairs so he knew that Davis was in full agreement with Johnson's policies of reconstruction. Moulton assured Johnson that most of "the honest portion of the American people" would approve of his pardoning Davis and view it as "reflecting further honor on your already historically-marked Administration."[30]

Next Davis secured testimonials in Jackson from Governor Benjamin G. Humphreys, William Yerger, and A. R. Johnston, all prominent former Whigs. Although they may have differed with him politically, they characterized Davis as a man of honor and integrity who would be loyal to the government whose flag "he so nobly defended in his youth."[31]

Joseph Davis's petition was then sent to Kentucky, where endorsements were added by Thomas E. Bramlette, governor of Kentucky, and Horatio Seymour, former governor of New York. In Cincinnati in May another petition recommended Davis for executive clemency considering "the extreme age, great suffering, pecuniary loss, and past services of the old man." This was signed by Senator James Guthrie of Kentucky, Washington McLean, editor of the *Cincinnati Enquirer,* and two others. On May 9 the printed petitions were presented to the president, who sent them on to O. O. Howard at the Freedmen's Bureau, asking "by what tenure the property of Mr. Davis is held by the Bureau of Refugees, Freedmen, and Abandoned Lands." After an exchange of telegrams with General Wood in Mississippi, where he determined that the plantations had never been legally confiscated, Howard replied on May 23 that Mr. Davis "should receive a pardon before being entitled to a restoration of his property."[32]

Friends of Joseph Davis now circulated one of the printed petitions in Washington. To the original signatures were added the names of twenty-four politicians of varied backgrounds, including prominent Democrats such as Senator Reverdy Johnson of Maryland, Senator Thomas A. Hendricks of Indiana and Montgomery Blair of Maryland along with his brother Francis P. Blair from Missouri. More surprising was the inclusion of such noted Republicans as Senator L. S. Trumbull of Illinois, Senator P. G. Van Winkle of West Virginia, and Representative Lovell H. Rousseau of Kentucky. On this first list of signers of the Davis petition, eighteen were Democrats and six were Republicans. This printed petition with five additional pages of signatures must have been presented to the president, too, although it is unclear what action resulted. Eventually, it was filed with other amnesty papers in the adjutant general's office.[33]

When no response to these efforts was forthcoming, Davis returned to writing letters. He drafted but seems not to have sent another communication to the president, again complaining of abuses by the bureau at Davis Bend. He claimed that "every means was used by the officers of the Bureau to discourage [the freedmen] from cultivating [their own lands] so as to enable them to supply labor to officers who were engaged in planting." He also complained that bureau agents were exploiting blacks by selling cheap goods and whiskey on the Bend. If an investigation were made by General James B. Steedman on his tour of the South, the old man promised that "startling abuses would be disclosed." Next Davis addressed a plea to an unlikely recipient, General U. S. Grant in Washington. He began, "I have long thought of writing to you. My defect of sight has prevented." Davis then described events during the war when he had believed General Grant's order promising that those who remained quietly at home would be undisturbed. He listed the abuses inflicted on people and property by the Freedmen's Bureau and told of his appeals to regain his lands. He concluded by asking Grant's aid to obtain an order from the president restoring his property, "for wasted as it is it may still be home for me and those dependent on me." There is no evidence that the general made any reply.[34]

In August Davis again addressed the president, saying that a friend who asked "Your Excellency" about the return of Davis's plantation last May was told that the bureau had no right to hold it unless it was abandoned property. Explaining that this was not the case, Davis said he had first been told that his property was held because he had refused to apply for a pardon and later that the bureau needed the land. He concluded by hoping that "even at this late day an order restoring my property" and the payment of the rents "will be received." At last the months of effort seemed to bear fruit. On September 8 Davis wrote to General Wood saying, "I have this day received my pardon from the Pres. of the Un. St. dated 28th March 1866." He requested the immediate return of Hurricane and Brierfield and removal of bureau agents "merchandising [there] . . . to the injury of the freedmen." Davis promised to protect the rights of those cultivating the plantations. Restoration of the property was not to be that easy, however. The Vicksburg office of the Freedmen's Bureau demanded evidence of Davis's special pardon, as well as proof of title to his estates. Furthermore, he was informed that lands under cultivation could not be restored without assurance that the cultivators would receive "a full & just compensation" for their labor. Without further orders from the president, the bureau officer claimed he could not return the Davis Bend property before the first of January 1867.[35]

Although all legal proof of his title had been destroyed during the war, Davis immediately secured sworn statements from Sheriff M. Shannon of Warren County and F. N. Steele, former tax assessor, attesting to his ownership of Hurricane and Brierfield. J. C. Chappell, clerk of the probate court, also swore to his ownership and certified that according to the records he had never sold any part of the plantations. As further evidence, Davis included a note from A. H. Arthur, cashier of the National Bank of Vicksburg, who stated that he had known Davis since 1835 and "there is no question about his ownership of said lands, as I have paid his taxes for them" from the Davis account. But even such proof was unavailing, and in his frustration, the elderly claimant drafted another bitter letter to the president, which he wisely decided not to send.[36]

Now Davis turned for assistance to a capable physician and loyal family friend, Dr. J. H. D. Bowmar, who was planning a trip to Washington, where he intended to try to get permission to visit Jefferson Davis in his Virginia prison. When he arrived in the capital city, Bowmar first consulted Commissioner Howard, asking for immediate restoration of Hurricane and Brierfield, but he was referred to President Johnson. As he subsequently reported, after waiting all day Bowmar finally succeeded in seeing the president alone at 10 P.M. on September 27. An embattled Johnson was suspicious of Howard's referral of the Davis case to him directly instead of through the usual channels via the secretary of war. Insisting that "this is a trick to get me into trouble," he told Bowmar to "take it back to Genl Howard & tell him to send it to Mr Stanton." The president also refused to grant him a permit to see the prisoner. Bowmar told Davis perceptively, "If Mr Johnson[']s star was in the ascendant he would not hesitate to put you in possession of your property at once but as it is he is afraid of his own shadow."[37]

Bowmar did not give up his efforts on Davis's behalf. The

next day he and Governor Sharkey decided that if they referred the case to Secretary of War Edwin M. Stanton he might revrese General Howard's restoration order. Instead, Bowmar again visited Howard to discuss the rents on the plantations. Howard claimed that Davis was entitled only to the amount that would accrue from September 8, when he received word of the presidential pardon. But after much discussion the persuasive Bowmar finally got him to agree to remit all the rents due from March 28, the date of the pardon. Sharkey was amazed at this achievement, and Davis later told a relative, "I am satisfied that [Bowmar] has done all that any one could have done & much better than most men could."[38]

Although the Freedmen's Bureau was reluctant to enrich Joseph Davis in any way and the Washington office warned Vicksburg officers repeatedly that "the Bureau is not to incur any outlay of money for Mr. Davis' benefit," all were finally forced to follow executive orders. Before the formal return of the property in January, General Wood gave Davis an $8,000 advance payment early in October, explaining to Howard that "it appeared as well that the money already collected should be in the hands of Mr. Davis as in the custody of government, with all the necessary risks." In November, Davis received an additional $9,000, and an unspecified final settlement was made after return of the plantations early in January.[39] His eighteen-month struggle was at last over, and Joseph Davis was no longer penniless. Given the attitude toward the Davis family in the victorious North, it is probably surprising that Joseph's compensation was so generous. Far from being grateful, the old man harbored only bitterness toward the government that still held his beloved brother in prison.

Recovery of his land brought no immediate change in Joseph Davis's way of life. He had no intention of trying to return to Davis Bend to rebuild the successful planting operation he had created there; he knew he lacked the strength for such an undertaking. But both his heart and his livelihood were still deeply involved in those plantations. He must find someone who would operate them with due regard for profit while respecting the interests of the former slaves, whom he still regarded as "his people." Although he had an offer from a northerner to buy both places, Davis easily made the decision to sell them instead to Ben Montgomery and his two sons, who were eager to own them.

There were several impediments to this action. First, it was illegal under the Mississippi Black Codes to sell rural property to blacks. To get around this law, Davis kept the sale contract secret and claimed publicly that he was leasing the land to the Montgomerys. Although this, too, was illegal, the Freedmen's Bureau had made it clear that the ban on black renting would not be enforced. Another problem was the Montgomerys' lack of capital for a down payment, but Davis decided to overlook this. He drew up a contract of sale for $300,000 due after nine years, with annual advance interest payments of 6 percent starting January 1, 1867. According to prices and customs of the time this was a fair contract, although during the next few years the annual payments of $18,000 proved to be burdensome as the price of cotton and land plummeted. Joseph Davis was a sympathetic and understanding creditor, however, and he modified the terms to fit the situation as long as he found his debtors working conscientiously.[40]

Other members of the family did not share Davis's confidence in the ability of the Montgomerys to operate the plantations successfully. When she visited Vicksburg earlier, Varina had expressed doubt about leasing to the blacks, and when he was informed of Joseph's plan to sell to them, Jefferson voiced similar skepticism. In a memorandum smuggled out of prison he suggested that the sale be completed as soon as possible "lest the desire for plunder & the active malignaty [sic] towards you as my brother should prompt to some Congressional movement to interfere with it." But he predicted that "unless the negroes exceed my expectations they will never complete the payments." He believed that, however able the Montgomerys had seemed thus far, "made lords of themselves I think they will rapidly lapse to the ignorance & vagrancy characteristic of their race." Joseph did not share his brother's low opinion of the blacks' capabilities. He had great faith in Ben Montgomery's ambition as well as his ability to manage his fellow freedmen. In February 1867, shortly after the governor of Mississippi signed a bill giving freedmen the right to own real property, Davis legally closed the sale contract with the Montgomerys. For the rest of his life the plantations at Davis Bend were a focus of his interest and profit rather than a major source of worry.[41]

The return of Hurricane and Brierfield did not bring an end to Davis's financial problems, however, nor did it stop his letter writing. Like all who had been prosperous planters before the war, he was enmeshed in the chaotic web created by the collapse of the southern financial system. Pressed by his creditors to pay antebellum debts immediately, he, in turn, brought all possible pressure on those who were indebted to him. With most of their buildings and equipment destroyed and their slaves freed, men of this class were in no position to pay their debts so that the economy could resume normal operations. In late 1865 the state legislature made an abortive effort to relieve debtors by enacting a law suspending all legal processes for the collection of debts until January 1, 1868, but the courts invalidated it within three months. The former Whigs who controlled the government opposed any abrogation of contract, regardless of postwar distress. No debtor relief was available to Mississippians until the Radical Republicans in Congress passed a general bankruptcy law in March 1867.

Joseph Davis had incurred many debts during the war and faced a number of postwar claims. He tried to avoid payment on most of them, thus contributing his share to the flood of lawsuits that deluged the courts. The largest claim against him was brought by Dr. T. J. Catchings for the balance of the money owed for Fleetwood, the plantation in Hinds County that Davis had bought as a refuge in 1862. Catchings had tried to back out of the agreement as soon as it was made and reluctantly accepted the first payment of $10,000 in Confederate currency. Now, after the destruction of all the buildings and equipment and loss of the livestock, Catchings refused to cancel Davis's note in exchange for the return of the land. A lifelong political opponent of the Davises, Catchings retained Joseph's enemy, Armistead Burwell, as his primary attorney, and the battle was joined. Starting in March 1866, the suit generated stacks of letters, depositions, and testimony about the charges and countercharges. In December 1867, Catchings was awarded a judgment of $6,000 and costs. Davis unsuccessfully appealed this decision, and by March 1869 the case was still pending. It cost Davis not only stiff legal fees to retain a team of six prominent lawyers in Jackson and Vicksburg but also a great deal of personal effort in building a defense. The zeal that he had formerly spent in drafting indignant letters to the president and government officials now was turned against some of his creditors.[42]

Davis was involved in many other lawsuits; in 1868 the circuit court of Warren County notified him of five cases against him in the December term alone. Some of these were for minor sums, such as the claim of Dr. E. G. Banks for $145 for medical services to slaves in 1862. A board of arbitration ruled that Davis must pay Banks $75 to settle this matter. Other disputes were not so easily handled. For example, Dr. A. L. McKay at first sought $235 for his services to the family and slaves in May 1863, but when Davis refused and made a counterclaim, McKay filed suit for $888. This case and the claim made by E. P. Smith involved debts incurred by Davis acting as agent for his brother during the refugee years; Davis generally refused to accept responsibility for these obligations. In a suit that stretched over four years he successfully avoided paying a $2,220 note that he had offered to settle during the war in Confederate bills.

Davis was also a creditor and strove just as earnestly to recover money owed him by others, but it was a difficult task. As he wrote his brother, "I had sold land to about seventy thousand dollars—the purchasers are either dead or broke—I get back the land, but it is unsaleable." For several years Davis tried through his attorneys to collect $45,390 owed him by James T. Rucks, who finally filed in bankruptcy, leaving Davis holding some poor land.

Even family members were not immune from dunning in these hard times. Davis wrote repeatedly to W. C. Van Benthuysen in New Orleans, asking him to repay more than $3,000 he had borrowed over the years. As Eliza Davis's nephew and a great favorite of hers, Van Benthuysen probably never expected to be called upon for restitution. But Eliza was dead and Davis was unrelenting in his demands, even recruiting his New Orleans factor, J. W. Payne, to attempt collection. Van Benthuysen, who was just getting started again in a postwar business, tried to keep their correspondence on a personal level by relating family news and urging Davis to stay with them when he visited New Orleans. By the end of 1867 he was able to start making small payments, which seemed to mollify Davis, and harmonious relations were eventually resumed.[43]

Some of Joseph Davis's former dependents, now adults, seemed remarkably inept at providing for themselves. Martha Harris, who was given to nervous headaches during their refugee years, turned up in Vicksburg, where she was upset to find that Davis could no longer support her and her adolescent daughter. His nephew Jeff Bradford stayed with Davis from time to time as he tried one job after another, always seeking something better. Davis confided to his brother that although the young man would probably make a living, he had "too much of the Bradford to pursue any thing with a steady purpose."[44]

Much more distressing was the behavior of Joe Nicholson, whom the Davises had raised from infancy. As early as 1866 he left unpaid hotel bills in Alabama, giving the impoverished Davis's name as guarantor. He returned to Vicksburg for a time and served as private secretary for Davis, whom he always called "Grandpa," but the next year in New Orleans he again borrowed money which he failed to repay. By April 1870 he was in trouble with authorities in New Orleans, apparently for forging drafts on Davis's account. The next month he was arrested and jailed in Jackson for forgery, and Davis gave up on him. He told Jefferson Davis, "[Nicholson's] utter recklessness would indicate insanity or almost inconceivable depravity. I do not feel disposed to attempt any thing for him." Nicholson may have been an alcoholic; he certainly was a disappointment to the elderly Davis.[45]

Other relatives tried to be helpful. At war's end Davis's nephew Hugh R. Davis, a fifty-year-old planter in West Feliciana Parish, Louisiana, heard from family members of Davis's poverty and placed some funds to his credit with Payne, Huntington and Co. in New Orleans. Although he appreciated the gesture, Joseph refused to accept the money, lecturing his nephew on the dangers of such benevolence. Citing the many demands of his immediate family on Hugh's resources, Davis warned that "so much generosity may be the cause of failure in the more important duties of your situation." Continuing his unsolicited advice, he added, "I believe the feeling [of] *Generosity* should not be inculcated in training the young, it is the generous that fail[,] it is the selfish that prosper in life, and who remembers the generous man after the power to be generous is gone." This seems strangely selfish advice from one who had a lifelong record of unfailing generosity to family and friends. He concluded, however, "It is worse to [be] *Mean* and this should be deeply impressed[,] *never do a mean thing.*"[46]

Davis was fond of most of his relatives and maintained a

lively interest in their welfare. He freely dispensed advice about making a living to men such as former son-in-law Dr. C. J. Mitchell, who seldom listened and usually failed to prosper. Davis warned against bringing the large Mitchell family from their impoverished farm in Texas to an equally unprofitable one across the river from Vicksburg. And when the physician as a last resort set up practice in town, Davis predicted that he would have many patients but few fees. For Davis, one of the greatest benefits of regaining his financial security was the return of his ability to lend a helping hand when he saw the need.

Besides the recovery of his plantations, Davis's greatest worry during the first postwar years was the fate of his beloved brother Jefferson. Eagerly gleaning what news filtered from the prison at Fortress Monroe, Joseph wrote often expressing his deep concern. Fulminating at the inhumane and unjust treatment of his brother, Davis was overjoyed to learn of his release in May 1867. Their reunion in Vicksburg was especially joyful for both of them; their affectionate relationship was a continual source of satisfaction to the brothers.

However the person closest to Davis, from Eliza's death until his own, was undoubtedly his devoted granddaughter Lise Mitchell, who was in almost constant attendance and always sensitive to his needs. She left him only briefly to make a trip to New Orleans in January 1866 to see her stepmother and small half-brothers and sisters who had recently arrived from Texas. She usually acted as her grandfather's companion and secretary, writing letters at his dictation and reading to him when his eyes grew tired. A devout Catholic, she seemed to get much satisfaction from her church activities and practiced Christian charity in her warm care of the elderly man who had raised her. Shortly after Joseph's death, Jefferson wrote to Lise, "Your sweet and exemplary devotion to your aged grandparent has long commanded my admiration and warmest thanks."[47]

Davis was not satisfied living in Vicksburg and from time to time considered moving elsewhere. To increase his mobility, his first purchase after receiving the rent money for his plantations was a carriage and horses to replace the mule and cart he had used all during the war. By the end of 1867 he had left Julia Porterfield's boardinghouse to occupy a large "house, stable and carriage house" he had rented at the corner of Cherry and Main streets. Here he could entertain in comfort the casual visitors who stopped by to chat of political and economic affairs over one of his Havana cigars, just as they had in his office at Hurricane. But the old man continued to be restless. Lise at first tried to persuade him to move to New Orleans, and when that failed she urged a return to Hurricane. Davis apparently never seriously considered going back because, as Jefferson told Lise, "On the plantation the annoyances would be much more frequent and the temptations to incur fatigue and exposure beyond his strength would increase daily."[48]

Joseph Davis resumed traveling as his financial condition improved. In 1868 he and Lise left Vicksburg for most of the summer. They made an even more extensive trip the next year, visiting nieces and their families in Kentucky and in Bethlehem, Pennsylvania. Sometime in late 1869, after his return to Vicksburg, Davis suffered a fall as he was alighting from his carriage. He dislocated his shoulder so severely that doctors decided not to try to set it immediately. He had planned to take Lise to New Orleans in February for Mardi Gras, but his injuries caused a postponement of the trip. Within a few weeks, he reported that he was dressed and "able to ride out" as before, and Lise said he was "almost himself again."[49]

Eventually he managed a visit to New Orleans, but the accident seemed to have dampened his spirits, and at age eighty-five he began to think about death. In April he directed Ben Montgomery to build a brick tomb for himself and his family in the Hurricane cemetery. In July, upon learning that his old enemy Armistead Burwell, whom he had "long known to be an unprincipled knave," would represent the plaintiff in a suit against him, he told his attorney, "Nothing but my feeble condition prevented me from applying to the court to have him struck off the role." In an August letter he described himself as "exhausted" and "feeble." In mid-September he took to his bed with an unspecified illness and died quietly in the early hours of Sunday, September 18, 1870. Dr. Bowmar later wrote, "He was perfectly conscious & his mind unimpaired up to within a few hours of his death."[50]

Since family members were so scattered, with the Jefferson Davises still in England, Lise and Joe Mitchell, perhaps at their grandfather's request, decided upon an immediate private funeral. The minister of Christ Church in Vicksburg gave up his usual Sunday service to join the small band of mourners who accompanied the body down the river to Hurricane. The afternoon funeral service there was attended primarily by Davis's friends in the black community. Some family friends later criticized the heirs for such a hasty interment, which precluded the large gathering and the Masonic rites to which Davis was entitled. However, it seems likely that Joseph Davis, a modest man, would have preferred the quiet Episcopal service at his grave under the trees beside his wife in the little family cemetery.

His death was widely reported in Mississippi newspapers. Noting that the remark frequently heard on Vicksburg streets was "Jeff. Davis' tutor is dead," the *Vicksburg Times* claimed that many regarded Joseph as "a man of greater abilities than his younger but more widely known brother," and it was "a commonly received opinion that it was from [Joseph] that the President received much of his political instruction." This obituary stressed the antebellum wealth and success enjoyed by the deceased and noted the "sincere sorrow" of the former Davis

Joseph E. Davis, ca. 1818
Portrait by William E. West
*Courtesy of Percival T. Beacroft, Jr., Rosemont Plantation, Woodville,
Mississippi*
Gift of Estate of Jefferson Hayes-Davis, grandson of President Jefferson Davis

Sketch of Vicksburg, Mississippi, in 1848
Old Courthouse Museum, Vicksburg, Mississippi

The black community at Hurricane Garden Cottage, Davis
Bend, ca. 1863
J. Mack Moore Collection, Old Courthouse Museum, Vicksburg, Mississippi

Eliza Van Benthuysen Davis, ca. 1859
Courtesy of Elizabeth Lorber

Joseph E. Davis, ca. 1859
Courtesy of Elizabeth Lorber

Jefferson and Varina Davis,
ca. 1867
Photograph by William
Notman, Montreal
*Courtesy of Eleanor S.
Brockenbrough Library, The
Museum of the Confederacy,
Richmond, Virginia*

Joseph E. Davis, ca. 1866
From a carte-de-visite in Varina Davis's collection
Photograph by Joslyn & Co., Washington Gallery, Vicksburg,
    Mississippi
*Courtesy of Eleanor S. Brockenbrough Library, The Museum of the
    Confederacy, Richmond, Virginia*

slaves at the loss of "'old man Joe'" to whom they "never appealed in vain when in trouble and distress."[51]

A longer and warmer obituary was written by his old friend General William H. McCardle for the *Vicksburg Herald* and reprinted in the *Weekly Clarion* in Jackson. McCardle stated that Davis's death "severs the last link between the Mississippi of the present, and Mississippi in its territorial condition." Tracing his life history (somewhat inaccurately), the editor reported that Davis was the last survivor of those who drew up the first Mississippi constitution in the 1817 convention, where he played a leading role. McCardle also remarked on his success as a lawyer among "the most brilliant minds of his day" and as a planter when "he amassed one of the finest estates in the country." Noting that as "a disciple of Jefferson," Joseph Davis was "a consistent and steadfast Democrat," McCardle regarded his foremost political achievement to be the development and training of his younger brother, "the greatest intellect of the age." The deceased was especially gifted "in the social circle," where he was "a most genial and fascinating companion." The article continued, "His intellect and his vast information, his quiet humor and kindly nature, combined to make him one of the most agreeable and entertaining gentlemen the writer has ever known." Although McCardle asserted that Davis was not perfect, he emphasized his unusual generosity to friends and family members. This obituary, like most of its time, stressed the good qualities of the dead man, yet there is the ring of truth in this testimonial of an old friend.[52]

Davis's heirs did not prosper as he must have hoped they would. There was one happy event: three years after her grandfather's death, Lise Mitchell at the age of thirty-one married William D. Hamer, an Alabama attorney whom she had known during their stay in Tuscaloosa. He had been crippled from childhood and walked with a cane so was exempt from military service. But he had been an attentive escort and good friend to Lise, who was sorry to part from him after the war. In 1876, when the Montgomerys encountered financial difficulties, the Hamers moved to Hurricane along with Joseph Mitchell and tried to make a living from the land Lise loved. She bore four children, two of whom died in infancy. Although Hamer died in 1880, she and her surviving children stayed on the plantation through floods and hard times till the turn of the century. However, these years were marred by family strife.

Joseph Davis's will failed to make specific disposition of Brierfield, the plantation he had given but never deeded to his brother. After acting as one of the executors for more than three years, Jefferson brought suit against the estate, claiming Brierfield was his alone. The ensuing lengthy litigation pitted Jefferson against Lise and Joe Mitchell and caused a permanent rift in the family. The two plantations were ultimately divided, but neither Joseph's brother nor his grandchildren benefited substantially from his legacy. Similar bitterness attended the suit brought by Davis's daughter Florida to overturn the provision of the will limiting her to a lifetime estate in Diamond Place. Unlike Jefferson, she was unsuccessful in her effort, and after her death in 1891 Joseph Mitchell inherited her plantation. In a perverse way, Joseph Davis, the patriarch, seemed to be reaching back from beyond the grave to maintain control of the land he prized so highly. And yet he surely would not have wished to bring pain and trouble to those he loved most dearly.[53]

In the rapidly industrializing America of 1870 Joseph Davis did, indeed, represent a link with the past. Born on the frontier of Georgia at the end of the American Revolution, he helped his parents struggle to clear a farm from the wilderness among hostile Indians. He shared the grass-roots American optimism that carried the growing Davis family across the Appalachians to start again several times in the newer lands of Kentucky. As a largely self-educated young man on the fresh Mississippi frontier he used his legal credentials to amass the fortune that enabled him to become a respected member of the landed gentry.

The chance that took him to the southwestern frontier of Mississippi instead of to land in the Northwest inevitably fixed his position in the slave society of the South. Had the Davises moved from Kentucky to Illinois, as did the Lincolns or the Shelbys, their wealth and political expertise undoubtedly would have served the Union rather than the Confederacy.

From his humble origins and his rearing in a society that prized self-help and individual responsibility, Joseph Davis derived values which he shared with his fellow citizens throughout the land. His patriotic devotion to the United States was as great as that of any contemporary New Englander. And his Christian concern for his fellow man was equally compelling. But like most successful men in the South, he found himself by mid-nineteenth century caught up in a system that required commitment to the "peculiar institution" as the price of maintaining his hard-earned wealth and status. He understood that slavery was inhumane and unjust, but his qualms of conscience as well as his belief in the increased efficiency of free labor were not strong enough to make him an abolitionist. Once hostilities began and his beloved brother became the leader of the Confederacy, Davis probably did not allow himself to reflect on the alternatives of an earlier generation.

This quintessential southern gentleman remained a very typical American in experience, values, and goals. Throughout his life he was a man on the move, ever searching for some better place or method or idea. His efforts to make a better life for himself, his extended family, his slaves and employees, his state, and his region helped in a small way to shape the nation. His life provides a personal vantage point from which to view nearly a century of American history.

NOTES

Abbreviations

BRFAL   Bureau of Refugees, Freedmen and Abandoned Lands

Davis, *Memoir* Varina Howell Davis, *Jefferson Davis, Ex-President of the Confederate States of America: A Memoir by his Wife.* 2 vols. New York, 1990.

LC   Library of Congress

MDAH   Mississippi Department of Archives and History

NA   National Archives

Papers   *The Papers of Jefferson Davis,* Haskell M. Monroe, Jr., and James T. McIntosh, eds., vol. 1, Baton Rouge, 1971; James T. McIntosh, ed., vol. 2, Baton Rouge, 1974, vol. 3, 1981; Lynda Laswell Crist, ed., vol. 4, Baton Rouge, 1983, vol. 5, 1985, vol. 6, 1989.

RG   Record Group

Chapter One

1. *Papers,* 1:8, n.11; Kirk Bentley Barb, "Extracts from the Genealogy of Jefferson Davis," reprinted ibid., 501–7; Walter L. Fleming, "The Early Life of Jefferson Davis," *Proceedings of the Mississippi Valley*

Historical Association 9 (1915–16):153–55; J. E. Davis to "My Dear Madam," June 30, 1866, Joseph E. Davis Papers, MDAH; For details of the local situation see Kenneth Coleman, *The American Revolution in Georgia, 1763–1789* (Athens, Ga., 1958).

2. Wilkes County, Ga., Land Grants, 1784–1839, Book GGG, p. 120, Book III, p. 249; Wilkes County, Ga., Deeds and Mortgages, Book DD, pp. 205–6, Book EE, pp. 169–70, both in Georgia Department of Archives and History, Atlanta; George Gilman Smith, *The Story of Georgia and the Georgia People* (Macon, 1900), 572; Fleming, "Early Life of Jefferson Davis," 154–55; Louise Frederick Hayes, *Hero of Hornet's Nest* (New York, 1946), 56–59, 173–74; Lucien Lamar Knight, comp., *Georgia's Roster of the Revolution* (Atlanta, 1920), 65, 258, 380; Alex M. Hitz, "Georgia Bounty Land Grants," *Georgia Historical Quarterly,* 38 (Dec. 1954):337–48.

3. Coleman, *American Revolution in Georgia,* 238–52; Hayes, *Hero of Hornet's Nest,* 202–4; Smith, *Story of Georgia,* 115.

4. Coleman, *American Revolution in Georgia,* 226; Eliza A. Bowen, *The Story of Wilkes County, Georgia* (Marietta, Ga., 1950), 46–48, 58; John Niven, *John C. Calhoun and the Price of Union* (Baton Rouge, 1988), 13–15; Margaret L. Coit, *John C. Calhoun* (Boston, 1950), 1, 9.

5. Bowen, *Wilkes County,* 33, 111–12, 115; Phillips Mill Baptist Church Records, Wilkes County, Ga., 1785–1948, microfilm, Historical Commission, Southern Baptist Convention, Nashville, Tenn.

6. Phillips Mill Baptist Church Records, 1785–1822; Bowen, *Wilkes County,* 131–34; Smith, *Story of Georgia,* 140; *Papers,* 1:512.

7. Bowen, *Wilkes County,* 17–18, 90, 134; Hayes, *Hero of Hornet's Nest,* 57–58, 313.

8. Harry A. Davis, *The Davis Family* (Washington, D.C., 1927), 38; Fleming, "Early Life of Jefferson Davis," 156; Stephen A. Channing, *Kentucky, A Bicentennial History* (New York, 1977), 71.

9. For accounts of this journey see Robert C. Kincaid, *The Wilderness Road* (New York, 1947), 160–95; [Harry Toulmin], *A Description of Kentucky in North America* (1792; rpt. Lexington, Ky., 1947), 94–95, 97, 117.

10. Willard Rouse Jillson, *The Kentucky Land Grants,* Filson Club Publications 33 (Louisville, Ky., 1925), 167; Jefferson Davis to Jerome

S. Ridley, Feb. 3, 1875, Jefferson Davis Papers, University of Alabama, Tuscaloosa; Mercer County Tax List, 1795, 1796, Kentucky Historical Society, Frankfort; Helen Bartter Crocker, *The Green River of Kentucky* (Lexington, Ky., 1976), 4–5, 9–10; Fleming, "Early Life of Jefferson Davis," 156.

11. Warren County, Ky., Deed Book 2, p. 89; Warren County, Ky., Tax Book, 1, 1797, p. 12, both in Kentucky Historical Society, Frankfort; Fleming, "Early Life of Jefferson Davis," 156.

12. Edward Coffman, *The Story of Logan County* (Nashville, 1962), 32–33, 41–42, 66–88; Crocker, *Green River,* 5–7, 11; John Boles, *The Great Revival, 1787–1805* (Lexington, Ky., 1972), 47–57.

13. Coffman, *Logan County,* 63, 82–83; Christian County Tax Book, 1800, Kentucky Historical Society, Frankfort; J. H. Battle and W. H. Perrin, eds., *Counties of Todd and Christian, Kentucky* (Chicago, 1884), 186–87; F. Garvin Davenport, *Ante-Bellum Kentucky* (Oxford, Ohio, 1943), 118–22.

14. Coffman, *Logan County,* 44, 130; Christian County, Ky., Tax Books, 1800, 1801, 1802, 1803; Christian County, Ky., Deed Book A, pp. 23–25; Warren County, Ky., Deed Book 2, p. 89; Fleming, "Early Life of Jefferson Davis," 156.

15. *Mirror* (Russellville, Ky.), Nov. 1, 1806.

16. Ibid.; Harriette Simpson Arnow, *Seedtime on the Cumberland* (New York, 1960), 407–8; Boynton Merrill, Jr., *Jefferson's Nephews* (Princeton, 1976), 135; Robert V. Remini, *Andrew Jackson and the Course of American Empire, 1767–1821* (New York, 1977), 132.

17. Christian County, Ky., Tax Books, 1805–9; James David Lynch, *The Bench and Bar of Mississippi* (New York, 1881), 73.

18. Michaux quotation in Thomas D. Clark, *Agrarian Kentucky* (Lexington, Ky., 1977), 9.

19. Channing, *Kentucky,* 40–43; N. S. Shaler, *Kentucky: A Pioneer Commonwealth* (Boston, 1884), 145–46; Christian County Tax Book, 1805, Kentucky Historical Society, Frankfort.

20. *Mirror* (Russellville, Ky.), Oct. 20, 1808; William Henry Perrin, ed., *Christian County of Kentucky* (Chicago, 1884), 86–87; H. Levin, ed., *The Lawyers and Lawmakers of Kentucky* (Chicago, 1897), 463; Merrill, *Jefferson's Nephews,* 176, 274; Coffman, *Logan County,* 25, 109–10;

Logan County Tax Book, 1806, Kentucky Historical Society, Frankfort; Jefferson Davis to Jerome Ridley, Feb. 3, 1875, Jefferson Davis Papers, University of Alabama.

21. Levin, *Lawyers,* 463; *Mirror* (Russellville, Ky.), Mar. 24, 1808; Remini, *Jackson,* 28–29; Coffman, *Logan County,* 106; Channing, *Kentucky,* 72–73; Clark, *Agrarian Kentucky,* 120–21.

22. *Mirror* (Russellville, Ky.), July 9, 1807; Coffman, *Logan County,* 127. For references to Davis's charm for women see transcript of Lynda Laswell's interview with V. Blaine Russell, July 31, 1972, Old Courthouse Museum, Vicksburg, Miss.; Mahala Eggleston Roach to her son, Aug. 22, 1897, Miscellaneous Manuscripts, MDAH.

23. Christian County Tax Books, 1805–9, Kentucky Historical Society, Frankfort; Fleming, "Early Life of Jefferson Davis," 157–58.

24. Register of Marriage of William Davis and Martha Crawford, Dec. 8, 1887, Gallatin County, Ill.; William Davis Bible owned by Joseph C. Lamb, Woodstown, N.J., copies of both documents furnished by Judie DaCostello, Reno, Nev. Although the letter from Jefferson Davis was destroyed, family tradition has convinced me that William was indeed Joseph's son.

25. Fleming, "Early Life of Jefferson Davis," 157–58; *Papers,* 1:8.

Chapter Two

1. Fortescue Cuming, "Cuming's Tour to the Western Country, 1807–1809," in Reuben Gold Thwaites, ed., *Early Western Travels, 1748–1846* (Cleveland, 1907), 4:331; James David Lynch, *The Bench and Bar of Mississippi* (New York, 1881), 73; J. F. H. Claiborne, *Mississippi as a Province, Territory and State* (Jackson, Miss., 1880), 1:357.

2. James Lal Penick, Jr., *The New Madrid Earthquakes* (Columbia, Mo., 1981); Mary Helen Dohan, *Mr. Roosevelt's Steamboat,* (New York, 1981), 124–28.

3. Dohan, *Mr. Roosevelt's Steamboat,* 162.

4. Cuming, "Tour to the Western Country," 315–17; Register of Appointments, County Officers, Series A, vol. N, pp. 154, 178, MDAH; Franklin L. Riley, "Extinct Towns and Villages of Mississippi," Mississippi Historical Society Publications 5 (1902): 345–46.

5. Richard A. McLemore, ed., *A History of Mississippi* (Jackson, Miss., 1973), 1:227; Claiborne, *Mississippi,* 1:331–32.

6. Mrs. Dunbar Rowland, "Mississippi Territory in the War of 1812," *Mississippi Historical Society Publications* 4 (1921): 17–37, 45–51.

7. Davis, Joseph, and Davis, Samuel, Hinds' Battalion, Cavalry, RG58 (War of 1812), M678, reel 14, MDAH; Rowland, "Mississippi Territory," 55–56.

8. Claiborne, *Mississippi*, 327–28; Rowland, "Mississippi Territory," 62–67; Davis, Joseph E., Davis, Samuel, Davis, Isaac W., Hinds' Battalion, Cavalry, RG58, M678, reel 14, MDAH.

9. Jefferson County, Miss., Personal Tax Rolls, 1815, 1816, 1817, MDAH; Mississippi Territory and Mississippi State Census Records, 1792–1866, Roll 547, Jefferson County, 1816, MDAH; *Reports of Cases in the Supreme Court of the State of Mississippi*, 2 Howard 786.

10. Clarence Edwin Carter, ed., *The Territorial Papers of the United States*, 6 (Washington, D.C., 1938), 709–12.

11. Claiborne, *Mississippi*, 275–76, 297–99; McLemore, ed., *History of Mississippi*, 208–16, 242–45; Carter, ed., *Territorial Papers*, 6: 712–17.

12. Cuming, "Tour to the Western Country," 319.

13. Claiborne, *Mississippi*, 259–60; Charles S. Sydnor, *A Gentleman of the Old Natchez Region* (Durham, N.C., 1938), 40–41.

14. William F. Winter, ed., "The Journal of the Constitutoinal Convention of 1817," *Journal of Mississippi History* 29 (Nov. 1967): 504; Mack Swearingen, *The Early Life of George Poindexter* (Chicago, 1934), 140–59; Winbourne Magruder Drake, "The Framing of Mississippi's First Constitution," *Journal of Mississippi History* 24 (Nov. 1967): 301–27.

15. Joseph E. Davis to Mrs. James Magill, Aug. 12, 1870, Jefferson Davis Association, Rice University, Houston, Tex.; Surveyor of U.S. Lands South of Tennessee, RG7, MDAH; Davis, *Memoir*, 1: 47–48.

16. Henry Bradshaw Fearon, *Sketches of America* (London, 1819), 271; *Journal of the House of Representatives of the State of Mississippi* (Natchez, 1820), 3d sess., 16–61, MDAH.

17. Dunbar Rowland, *History of Mississippi: The Heart of the South* (Chicago, 1925), 2: 615–16.

18. Cuming, "Tour to the Western Country," 319; John James Audubon, *Delineations of American Scenery and Character* (New York, 1926), 332–35; D. Clayton James, *Antebellum Natchez* (Baton Rouge, 1968), 3–76, 114; Sydnor, *Gentleman of Old Natchez*, 22, 72, 128.

19. James, *Antebellum Natchez,* 257; Robert E. May, *John A. Quitman, Old South Crusader* (Baton Rouge, 1985), 22.

20. *Mississippi State Gazette* (Natchez), April 7, 1820.

21. Claiborne, *Mississippi,* 358; Michael de L. Landon, "The Mississippi State Bar Association, 1821–1825: The First in the Nation," *Journal of Mississippi History* 42 (Aug. 1980): 227, 239; Adams County Tax Rolls, 1820–25, MDAH.

22. Landon, "Mississippi State Bar Association," 222–42; Jefferson Davis v. J. H. D. Bowmar, et al., Warren County Chancery Court, July 3, 1874–Jan. 8, 1876, unreported, p. 471, MDAH.

23. Lynch, *Bench and Bar,* 74–75; Hudson Strode, *Jefferson Davis, American Patriot, 1808–1861* (New York, 1955), 110.

24. Adams County, Miss., Deed Books M, pp. 325–27, N, p. 129, O, pp. 39, 186, 215, 315–16, and P, pp. 374–75; Adams County Tax Rolls, 1821–25; Fiscal Records, vol. 78, all in MDAH; "Grand Lodge of Mississippi," Old Court House Museum, Vicksburg; Joseph Dunbar Shields, *Natchez: Its Early History* (Louisville, Ky., 1930), 248; *Port Gibson Correspondent,* Sept. 13, 1822; Sydnor, *Gentleman of Old Natchez,* 130; James, *Antebellum Natchez,* 228, 232, 242, 248–49.

25. *Mississippi State Gazette,* April 2, 23, 1825.

26. Davis maintained contact with Wright; two years later she visited the Davis plantation and left a troublesome slave under Joseph's supervision. See A. J. G. Perkins and Theresa Wolfson, *Frances Wright: Free Enquirer* (New York, 1939), 192; Cecilia Morris Eckhardt, *Fanny Wright: Rebel in America* (Cambridge, Mass., 1984), 86–107, 145.

27. *Papers,* 1:11–13, 17–18, 124.

28. Landon, "Mississippi Bar Association," 237, 241.

29. *Papers,* 2:54, 124, 330, 4:402; *The Diaries of Donald Macdonald, 1824–1826,* Indiana Historical Society Publications no. 2 (Indianapolis, 1942), 298; Strode, *Jefferson Davis, Patriot,* 39.

30. *Diaries of Macdonald,* 299; Margaret Cole, *Robert Owen of New Lanark* (New York, 1953), 148–49; A. E. Bestor, *Backwoods Utopias* (Philadelphia, 1950), 104–14; Davis, *Memoir,* 1:49–50, 171–72.

31. *Diaries of Macdonald,* 299–300; Daniel J. Boorstin, *The Americans: The National Experience* (New York, 1965), 254–55; *Papers,* 1:30; Davis, *Memoir,* 1:49–51.

32. James, *Antebellum Natchez*, 115.

33. Register of County Appointments, Warren County, MDAH; M. E. Hamer to W. L. Fleming, Jan. 30, 1908, Walter Lynwood Fleming Collection, New York Public Library; Davis, *Memoir*, 1:48.

34. For Quitman's life see May, *Quitman*.

35. *Papers*, 1:272, 4:402–3; Adams County Marriage Records, Book 5, p. 93, MDAH; *Washington Republican*, Aug. 18, 1813; Strode, *Jefferson Davis, Patriot*, 51.

Chapter Three

1. Davis, *Memoir*, 1:163, 202–3, 475; Frank E. Everett, Jr., *Brierfield: Plantation Home of Jefferson Davis* (Hattiesburg, Miss., 1971), 7–9.

2. Eliza Davis to Jefferson Davis, Nov. 17, 1834, Jefferson Davis Papers, Transylvania University, Lexington, Ky.

3. Mahala Eggleston Roach to Thomas Robins Roach, Aug. 22, 1897, Miscellaneous Manuscripts, MDAH; Davis, *Memoir*, 1:192–93; Mary Mitchell White, "Interludes," 167, typescript, in possession of Betty White Wells, Tulsa, Okla.; William Wood, *The Autobiography of William Wood* (New York, 1895), 1:456–57.

4. Letter fragment from Joseph Davis, Oct. 9, 1865, Joseph Davis Papers, MDAH; Joseph Davis to Jefferson Davis, Feb. 13, 1847, Museum of the Confederacy, Richmond, Va.

5. M. E. Hamer to W. L. Fleming, Jan. 30, 1908, Walter Lynwood Fleming Collection, New York Public Library.

6. U.S. Census, 1830, 1840, 1850, 1860, Warren County, Miss., and Personal Tax Rolls, 1828–61, Warren County, Miss., MDAH; Gavin Wright, *The Political Economy of the Cotton South* (New York, 1978), 46–47; Peter Temin, *The Jacksonian Economy* (New York, 1969), 103; Kenneth M. Stampp, *The Peculiar Institution* (New York, 1956), 408–9.

7. James David Lynch, *The Bench and Bar of Mississippi* (New York, 1881), 76; Davis, *Memoir*, 1:174; *Farmer's Register* 5(1835): 32. For a detailed treatment of the slave community at Davis Bend see Janet Sharp Hermann, *The Pursuit of a Dream* (New York, 1981).

8. Davis, *Memoir*, 1:174; M. E. Hamer to W. L. Fleming, Jan. 30, 1908, Fleming Collection. For other masters who gave their slaves

similar incentives see John Hebron Moore, *The Emergence of the Cotton Kingdom in the Old Southwest* (Baton Rouge, 1988), 100–103.

9. Davis, *Memoir,* 1 : 176–77.

10. Ibid., 179, 193; W. L. Fleming, "Jefferson Davis, the Negroes and the Negro Problem," *Sewanee Review* 16 (Oct. 1908): 407–27.

11. Charles Sydnor, *Slavery in Mississippi* (Baton Rouge, 1966), 149, 165–66; Warren County Tax Rolls, 1836, MDAH. Details of Montgomery's early life are found in his son's account, *New York World,* Sept. 28, 1890, and *New Orleans Times Democrat,* Feb. 18, 1902; see also Hermann, *Pursuit,* 17–22.

12. *New York World,* Sept. 28, 1890.

13. Joseph Davis letter fragment, Oct. 9, 1865, Joseph Davis Papers, MDAH.

14. Roach to son, Aug. 22, 1897, Miscellaneous Manuscripts, MDAH; Hamer to Fleming, Jan. 30, 1908, Fleming Papers; Davis, *Memoir,* 1 : 174–75; Ben Montgomery to Joseph Davis, June 27, 1866, Joseph Davis Papers, MDAH.

15. Isaiah T. Montgomery Pension Record, Civil War, XC2997096, Washington National Records Center, Suitland, Md.; Roach to son, Aug. 22, 1897, MDAH. For a detailed account of the Montgomery family see Hermann, *Pursuit.*

16. Isaiah Montgomery to Booker T. Washington, Jan. 29, 1909, Booker T. Washington Papers, LC.

17. D. Clayton James, *Antebellum Natchez* (Baton Rouge, 1968), 175.

18. James, *Antebellum Natchez,* 175–76; Marie T. Morgan, *Mississippi-Louisiana Border Country: A History of Rodney, Miss., St. Joseph, La., and Environs* (Baton Rouge, 1970), 187–90; Isaiah Montgomery to Booker T. Washington, Jan. 29, 1909, Washington Papers; Joseph Davis to Senator Henry Wilson, Dec. 24, 1865, BRFAL, National Archives Microfilm Publication M826, reel 16.

19. *Joseph E. Davis* v. *Rice C. Ballard et al.,* RG 8, Superior Court of Chancery case no. 3973, MDAH; *Laws of Mississippi* (Jackson, 1846), 172–73; *Papers,* 3 : 122.

20. *R. C. Ballard et al.* v. *Joseph E. Davis,* 31 Miss. 525, 535 (1856), 535–37.

21. *Joseph E. Davis* v. *Benjamin Sanders et al.,* RG8, Superior Court of

Chancery case no. 4685, MDAH; Jefferson Davis to Major Campbell Brown, June 14, 1886, Jefferson Davis Manuscripts, Huntington Library, San Marino, Calif.

22. Wood, *Autobiography,* 1:456–57; Mama (Eliza Davis) to Mrs. Charles J. Mitchell, Feb. 17, 1846, Mary Elizabeth Mitchell Book, Southern Historical Collection, University of North Carolina, Chapel Hill.

23. Varina Davis to "My dear Mother," Dec. 13, 1847, Jefferson Davis Papers, University of Alabama, Tuscaloosa; "Warren County Marriages," *Journal of Mississippi History* 28 (Nov. 1966): 326, 29 (Aug. 1967): 214.

24. Florida (Davis McCaleb) to Jefferson Davis, June 30, 1833, *Papers,* 1:272, 2:64–66.

25. *Papers,* 1:304; Mary Lucinda Davis to Ellen Mary Davis, Nov. 27, 1837, in possession of Percival T. Beacroft, Jr., Woodville, Miss.

26. Mary Davis Mitchell to Mrs. Joseph E. Davis, Dec. 5, 1838, Mitchell Book, Southern Historical Collection: Mary Davis Mitchell to Lucy Bradford, Feb. 9, 1845, Lise Mitchell Papers, Tulane University, New Orleans.

27. *Papers,* 1:303, 470.

28. *Papers,* 2:4–6, 18–19.

29. Varina Davis to Mrs. Howell, Dec. 13, 1847, Jefferson Davis Papers, University of Alabama; *Vicksburg Daily Whig,* Dec. 5, 1856.

30. For Joseph Nicholson's history see *Papers,* 2:14–15. The background of Martha Quarles Harris is taken from her obituary in the *Vicksburg Evening Post,* May 5, 1889, and Everett, *Brierfield,* 151. David Bradford's murder is described in the *Richmond* (La.) *Compiler,* March 15, 1844; see also *Papers,* 2:128–29, 3:100, 4:411–14.

31. Davis, *Memoir,* 1:163, 172; *Papers,* 1:lxxviii, 246.

32. *Papers,* 3:301–3; see also 2:53, 3:96.

33. Jefferson Davis v. J. H. D. Bowmar et al.; Warren County Chancery Court, July 3, 1874–Jan. 8, 1876, unreported, pp. 346–47, 354–56, MDAH; Varina Davis to Margaret Howell, Jan., Dec. 13, 1847, July 22, 1851, Feb. 9, May 25, 1852, Varina Davis to Mr. and Mrs. Howell, Oct. 28, 1851, all in Jefferson Davis Papers, University of Alabama.

34. *Papers,* 1:303, 342; Eliza Davis to Rev. J. F. Young, Sept. 22, 1851, John Freeman Young Papers, Southern Historical Collection, University of North Carolina, Chapel Hill.

35. Davis v. Bowmar, 349, 359–68, 383, 469; *Papers,* 5:111–12; Varina Davis to Margaret Howell, [no month] 24, 1849, Oct. 28, 1851, Feb. 9, March 4, May 25, 1852, April 29, 1854, Jefferson Davis Papers, University of Alabama.

36. *Papers,* 1:448–49.

37. John Randolph to Jefferson Davis, Sept. 10, 1839, in possession of Joel A. H. Webb, Colorado Springs, Colo.; Florida Davis McCaleb to Jefferson Davis, July 19, 1838, *Papers,* 1:448.

38. There are references to the health of family members in many letters in all volumes of the *Papers.*

39. Joseph E. Davis to Dr. C. J. Mitchell, July 21, 1849, Mitchell Book, Southern Historical Collection; *Papers,* 4:402–16.

40. Zachary Taylor to Jefferson Davis, April 18, 1848, incomplete draft, Zachary Taylor Papers, LC.

41. Eliza Davis to Rev. J. F. Young, Sept. 22, 1851, Young Papers; Varina Davis to Margaret Howell, July 22, 1851, Jefferson Davis Papers, University of Alabama.

42. *Papers,* 1:464–65.

43. Hudson Strode, *Jefferson Davis: Private Letters, 1823–1889* (New York, 1966), 80; Zachary Taylor to Jefferson Davis, April 18, July 10, 1848, Taylor Papers; *Papers,* 1:448–51.

44. *Papers,* 6:667; Charles S. Sydnor, *A Gentleman of the Old Natchez Region* (Durham, N.C., 1938), 262–65, 274; Joseph E. Davis Overseer Report, [1833], Natchez Trace Collection, Eugene C. Barker Texas History Center, Austin, Texas.

45. *Vicksburg Weekly Whig,* Dec. 14, 1859.

46. Sydnor, *Gentleman of Old Natchez,* 266–73; *Papers,* 1:432–33; Daniel J. Boorstin, *The Americans: The National Experience* (New York, 1965), 100–101.

47. *Papers,* 6:258, 612.

48. Eliza Davis to Jefferson Davis, July 15, 1859, Jefferson Davis Papers, University of Alabama.

49. Eliza Davis to Jefferson Davis, July 29, 1859, ibid.

50. Eliza Davis to Jefferson Davis, July 29, 1859, ibid.; *Davis* v. *Bowmar*, 367; Strode, *Jefferson Davis, Patriot*, 335.

51. Davis, *Memoir*, 1:171; Strode, *Jefferson Davis, Patriot*, 111; *Woodville Republican*, Sept. 24, 1842.

52. Edwin Arthur Miles, *Jacksonian Democracy in Mississippi* (Chapel Hill, 1960), 36–37; *Papers*, 1:246; Robert E. May, *John A. Quitman, Old South Crusader* (Baton Rouge, 1985), 50–57; *Vicksburg Tri-Weekly Sentinel*, Oct. 28, 1839; Davis, *Memoir*, 1:171–72; Strode, *Jefferson Davis, Patriot*, 111.

53. *Papers*, 1:437–38, 2:11; *Vicksburg Register*, July 9, 16, 30, 1835; Edwin C. Miles, "The Mississippi Slave Insurrection Scare of 1835," *Journal of Negro History* 42 (Jan. 1957): 48–60; Bertram Wyatt-Brown, *Southern Honor: Honor, Ethics, and Behavior in the Old South* (New York, 1982), 348–49; Miles, *Jacksonian Democracy*, 123–24.

54. *Vicksburg Sentinel*, June 5, 1844.

55. Wyatt-Brown, *Southern Honor*, 350–61; Henry Stuart Foote, *A Casket of Reminiscences* (Washington, D.C., 1874), 186; Marion Bragg column, *Vicksburg Evening Post*, Nov. 25, 1972; Boorstin, *Americans*, 206–12.

56. *Woodville Republican*, Sept. 24, 1842; *Papers*, 2:240–41.

57. *Papers*, 3:164–65, 172–73, 4:124n. For an excellent account of the Taylor campaign and administration see William J. Cooper, Jr., *The South and the Politics of Slavery, 1828–1856* (Baton Rouge, 1978), 245–78.

58. *Papers*, 1:464–65, 2:239–42, 4:300–301. For the political activities of both Davises see *Papers*, passim, and newspapers from Vicksburg and Jackson, 1840–60.

59. A. G. Brown to J. F. H. Claiborne, Dec. 19, 1855, John F. H. Claiborne Collection, MDAH; *Southern Reformer*, June 28, 1845; *Papers*, 1:465.

60. *Yazoo Whig and Political Register*, Sept. 12, Oct. 28, 1842; *South-Western Farmer* (Raymond Miss.), Sept. 16, 30, 1842; *Woodville Republican*, Sept. 24, 1842; *Jackson Mississippian*, Oct. 27, 1850; *Jackson Semi-Weekly Mississippian*, Dec. 29, 1854; *DeBow's Review of the Southern & Western States* 15 (Sept. 1853): 254–74; 17 (Dec. 1854): 91–99, 200–213; Jere W. Roberson, "The Memphis Commercial Convention of 1853," *Tennessee Historical Quarterly* 33 (1974): 279–96.

61. Bettie Bradford to Nannie, Dec. 21, 1853, Lise Mitchell Papers; Lynch, *Bench and Bar,* 75; *Papers,* 2:12.

Chapter Four

1. Davis, *Memoir,* 2:4–5, 9–10.

2. Joseph Davis to Jefferson Davis, Jan. 2, 1861, Jefferson Davis Papers, LC; Percy Lee Rainwater, *Mississippi, Storm Center of Secession, 1856–1861* (Baton Rouge, 1938), 168–69. For the secession movement in Mississippi, in addition to Rainwater, see William L. Barney, *The Secessionist Impulse: Alabama and Mississippi in 1860* (Princeton, 1974). The Mississippi secession convention is well covered in Ralph A. Wooster, *The Secession Conventions of the South* (Princeton, 1962), 26–48. For Jefferson Davis's role see Clement Eaton, *Jefferson Davis* (New York, 1977), 115–27.

3. Joseph Davis to Andrew Johnson, Sept. 22, 1865, BRFAL, M826, reel 9, LC; Jefferson Davis v. J. H. D. Bowmar et al., Warren County Chancery Court, July 3, 1874–Jan. 8, 1876, unreported, pp. 446, MDAH.

4. Jefferson Davis to Joseph Davis, June 18, 1861, in possession of Mrs. J. D. Marrett, Smithfield, Ky.; Gignel and Jameson to Joseph Davis, Nov. 23, 1866, Joseph Davis Papers, MDAH.

5. C. Vann Woodward, ed., *Mary Chesnut's Civil War* (New Haven, 1981), 79–123; Lise Mitchell Journal, July n.d. 1862, Tulane University, New Orleans.

6. Lise Mitchell Journal, July n.d., 1862.

7. Woodward, ed., *Mary Chesnut's Civil War,* 119–55; Davis, *Memoir,* 2:41–47, 94; Lise Mitchell Journal, July n.d., 1862.

8. Lise Mitchell Journal, July n.d., 1862; Eliza Davis to Martha Harris, Aug. 10, 1861, Lise Mitchell Papers, Tulane University, New Orleans.

9. Woodward, ed., *Mary Chesnut's Civil War,* 90, 127; Davis, *Memoirs,* 2:198–99; Lise Mitchell Journal, July n.d., 1862.

10. Lise Mitchell Journal, July n.d., 1862.

11. Lise Mitchell Journal, Tulane University; James M. McPherson, *Ordeal by Fire: The Civil War and Reconstruction* (New York, 1982), 217–18.

12. Jefferson Davis to Joseph Davis, Feb. 21, 1862, in *Washington Daily Morning Chronicle,* May 13, 1864; Joseph Davis to Jefferson Da-

vis, April 20, 1862, Jefferson Davis Papers, Transylvania University, Lexington, Ky.; Lise Mitchell Journal, Tulane University.

13. Joseph Davis to Jefferson Davis, April 21, 22, June 18, 1862, Jefferson Davis Papers, Transylvania University.

14. Joseph Davis to Jefferson Davis, May 2, 1862, Jefferson Davis Papers, Transylvania University; Lise Mitchell Journal, July n.d., 1862.

15. Lise Mitchell Journal, July n.d., 1862; Joseph Davis to Jefferson Davis, May 2, June 18, 1862, Jefferson Davis Papers, Transylvania University.

16. Joseph Davis to Jefferson Davis, May 2, 1862, Jefferson Davis Papers, Transylvania University; Samuel Carter III, *The Final Fortress: The Campaign for Vicksburg, 1862–1863* (New York, 1980), 26–39; Davis v. Bowmar, 398, MDAH; *Papers,* 4:293; Lise Mitchell Journal, July n.d., 1862.

17. Joseph Davis to Jefferson Davis, May 2, 22, 1862, Jefferson Davis Papers, Transylvania University.

18. Joseph Davis to Jefferson Davis, May 22, 1862, Jefferson Davis Papers, Transylvania University.

19. Joseph Davis to Jefferson Davis, June 13, 1862, in possession of Adele Hayes-Davis Davis, Colorado Springs, Colo.; Hudson Strode, *Jefferson Davis, Confederate President* (New York, 1959), 262–63.

20. Joseph Davis to Jefferson Davis, June 6, 18, 1862, Jefferson Davis Papers, Transylvania University; *Vicksburg Daily Whig,* June 6, 1862; *Hinds County Gazette,* June 18, 25, 1862; Joseph Davis to Andrew Johnson, Sept. 22, 1865, M826, reel 9, NA.

21. Strode, *Jefferson Davis, President* 287; M. L. Smith to Jefferson Davis, telegram, June 26, 1862, Jefferson Davis Papers, Duke University, Durham, N.C.

22. Joseph Davis to Jefferson Davis, June 13, 18, 22, July 10, Aug. 31, 1862, Jefferson Davis Papers, Transylvania University; Joseph Davis to Jefferson Davis, Aug. 23, 1862, Jefferson Davis Papers, University of Alabama, Tuscaloosa; Dr. Banks Account, June–Aug. 1862, Joseph Davis Papers, MDAH; Eliza Davis to Jefferson Davis, Aug. 24, 1862, Jefferson Davis Papers, Tulane University.

23. Joseph Davis to Jefferson Davis, May 22, 1862, Jefferson Davis Papers, Transylvania University.

24. Joseph Davis to Jefferson Davis, Sept. 22, 1862, ibid.

25. Joseph Davis to Jefferson Davis, May 22, June 18, Aug. 31, Sept. 22, Oct. 7, 1862, ibid.; Joseph Davis to Jefferson Davis, Aug. 23, 1862, Jefferson Davis Papers, University of Alabama; Eliza Davis to Jefferson Davis, Aug. 24, 1862, Jefferson Davis Papers, Tulane University, New Orleans.

26. Joseph Davis to Jefferson Davis, Oct. 29, Nov. 1, 21, 1862, Jefferson Davis Papers, Transylvania University.

27. Answer of Thomas J. Catchings to the Cross Bill of Joseph E. Davis . . . , No. 227 in Warren County Chancery Court, Dec. 14, 1868, in Joseph Davis Papers, MDAH; Joseph Davis to Jefferson Davis, Nov. 1, 21, 1862, Jefferson Davis Papers, Transylvania University.

28. Answers of O. B. Cox to Interrogatories, Catchings v. Davis, Joseph Davis Papers, MDAH.

29. Answer of Thomas J. Catchings to Cross Bill of Joseph E. Davis, Answers of O. B. Cox to Interrogatories, Answers of Joseph E. Davis to original and supplemental Bills of Complaints, Catchings v. Davis; William Yerger to Joseph E. Davis, Feb. 21, 1867; E. L. Miles to Joseph Davis, May 27, 1867, all in Joseph Davis Papers, MDAH.

30. Answers of Joseph E. Davis to original and supplemental Bills of Complainant, Catchings v. Davis, Joseph Davis Papers, MDAH; Joseph Davis to Jefferson Davis, Nov. 27, 1862, Jefferson Davis Papers, Transylvania University.

31. Answer of Thomas J. Catchings to Cross Bill of Joseph E. Davis, Catchings v. Davis, Joseph E. Davis Papers, MDAH; Lise Mitchell Journal, March 1863.

32. Joseph Davis to Jefferson Davis, Oct. 7, Nov. 27, 1862, Jefferson Davis Papers, Transylvania University; Carter, *Final Fortress,* 81–82, 89–90, 94–95, 97–98; Lise Mitchell Journal.

33. Joseph Davis to Jefferson Davis, Feb. 17, 1863, in possession of Adele Hayes-Davis Davis, Colorado Springs, Colo.

34. Joseph Davis to Jefferson Davis, June 18, Oct. 7, 29, Nov. 1, 21, 27, 1862, Jefferson Davis Papers, Transylvania University; Joseph Davis to Jefferson Davis, Feb. 17, 1863, in possession of Adele Hayes-Davis Davis, Colorado Springs, Colo.

35. Joseph Davis to Jefferson Davis, May 7, 1863, Jefferson Davis Papers, Transylvania University, Lise Mitchell Journal, Aug. 1864.

36. Joseph Davis to President Andrew Johnson, Sept. 22, 1865, BRFAL, M826, reel 9, LC.

37. Ibid.; Lise Mitchell Journal, Aug. 1864; Carter, *Final Fortress,* 181–94.

38. Joseph Davis to President Andrew Johnson, Sept. 22, 1865, BRFAL, M826, reel 9, LC.

39. Joseph Davis to Jefferson Davis, June 3, 1863, Jefferson Davis Papers, Transylvania University; Joseph Davis to President Andrew Johnson, Sept. 22, 1865, BRFAL, M826, reel 9, LC; Lise Mitchell Journal, Aug. 1864; Carter, *Final Fortress,* 195; William C. Harris, *Presidential Reconstruction in Mississippi* (Baton Rouge, 1967), 196.

40. Lise Mitchell Journal, Aug. 1864.

41. Joseph Davis to Jefferson Davis, June 3, 7, 14, 17, 21, 1863, Jefferson Davis Papers, Transylvania University; Lise Mitchell Journal, Aug. 1864.

42. E. J. Harvie to J. E. Davis, June 21, 1863, Army of Tennessee, Letters Sent; J. E. Davis to the President, telegrams, June 14, 22, 1863, all in Jefferson Davis Papers, RG109, NA.

43. Joseph Davis to Jefferson Davis, June 3, 14, 17, 21, 25, 1863, Jefferson Davis Papers, Transylvania University.

44. E. J. Harvie to J. E. Davis, June 21, 1863, Army of Tennessee, Letters Sent; J. E. Davis to the President, telegrams, June 14, 22, 24, 25, all in Jefferson Davis Papers, RG 109, NA; Jefferson Davis to Joseph Davis, May 7, 31, 1863, Lise Mitchell Papers.

45. Lise Mitchell Journal, Aug. 1864.

46. Lise Mitchell to Nannie [Anna Bradford Miles], Aug. 20, 1863, Lise Mitchell Papers; Lise Mitchell Journal, Aug. 1864.

47. Joseph Davis to Jefferson Davis, Sept. 9, 28, 1863, Jefferson Davis Papers, Transylvania University; Lise Mitchell Journal, Aug. 1864.

48. Joseph Davis to Jefferson Davis, Aug. 15, Sept. 9, 16, 28, 1863, Jefferson Davis Papers, Transylvania University; Lise Mitchell Journal, Aug. 1864; Jefferson D. Bradford to Jefferson Davis, Aug. 17, 1863, Jefferson Davis Papers, Museum of the Confederacy, Richmond, Va.; Robert Melvin to Jefferson Davis, July 22, 1863, Jefferson Davis Papers, Duke University; *New York Times,* Aug. 2, 1863.

49. Jefferson Davis to Joseph Davis, May 31, 1863; Lise Mitchell

Papers; Joseph Davis to Jefferson Davis, Aug. 15, 1863, Jefferson Davis Papers, Transylvania University.

50. Joseph Davis to Jefferson Davis, Sept. 16, Nov. 1, 4, 11, Dec. 1, 1863, Jefferson Davis Papers, Transylvania University; Jefferson Davis to Joseph Davis, May 31, 1863, Lise Mitchell Papers.

51. Lise Mitchell Journal, Aug. 1864; Joseph Davis to Jefferson Davis, Nov. 11, Dec. 1, 1863, Jefferson Davis Papers, Transylvania University.

52. Joseph Davis to Jefferson Davis, April 8, 1864, in possession of Adele Hayes-Davis Davis, Colorado Springs, Colo.; Lise Mitchell Journal, Aug. 1864; Joseph Davis to Jefferson Davis, Dec. 1, 1863, Jefferson Davis Papers, Transylvania University; Joseph Davis to President Andrew Johnson, Sept. 22, 1865, BRFAL, M826, reel 9, NA.

53. Joseph Davis to Jefferson Davis, April 23, May 10, 1864, Jefferson Davis Papers, Transylvania University.

54. Joseph Davis to Jefferson Davis, March 19, 1865, Jefferson Davis Papers, Transylvania University; Joseph Davis to Jefferson Davis, April 8, 1865, Jefferson Davis Papers, University of Alabama; Lise Mitchell Journal, Feb. 1865.

55. Elizabeth Avery Meriwether, *Recollections of 92 Years, 1824–1916* (Nashville, 1958), 127–29; Lise Mitchell Journal, Feb. 1865; Mary Elizabeth Massey, *Refugee Life in the Confederacy* (Baton Rouge, 1964), 174.

56. Joseph Davis to Jefferson Davis, March 19, 1865, Jefferson Davis Papers, Transylvania University.

57. Lise Mitchell Journal, April, May, June, July 1865.

58. Lise Mitchell Journal, March 1867; Joseph E. Davis Loyalty Oath, July 7, 1865, Natchez Trace Collection, Eugene C. Barker History Center, University of Texas, Austin; Joseph E. Davis to Andrew Johnson, Sept. 22, 1865, BRFAL, M826, reel 9, NA.

Chapter Five

1. William C. Harris, *Presidential Reconstruction in Mississippi* (Baton Rouge, 1967), 73; Lise Mitchell Journal, March 1867, Tulane University, New Orleans.

2. Harris, *Presidential Reconstruction,* 19, 68, 72–73, 218; Lise Mitchell Journal, March 1867.

3. Harris, *Presidential Reconstruction,* 19, 31, 220–22; Lise Mitchell Journal, March 1867; Ben Montgomery to Joseph Davis, Oct. 14, 1865, Joseph Davis Papers, MDAH.

4. Nellie D. Dupree, "Some Historic Homes of Mississippi," Mississippi Historical Society *Publications* 7 (1902): 252–53; *Papers,* 2:64–65.

5. For a detailed description of the struggle with federal authorities from the Montgomerys' viewpoint see Janet Sharp Hermann, *The Pursuit of a Dream* (New York, 1981), 66–106.

6. Benjamin Montgomery to Joseph E. Davis, Oct. 14, 1865, Joseph Davis Papers, MDAH; Joseph E. Davis to Colonel Samuel Thomas, Oct. 21, 1865, M826, reel 9, and Joseph Davis Papers, MDAH; Joseph E. Davis to General O. O. Howard, Oct. 27, 1865, M826, reel 10, NA.

7. Joseph E. Davis to Samuel Thomas, Oct. 21, 1865, enclosing report of John T. Donaly, Oct. 17, 1865, M826, reel 9, NA.

8. Davis to Thomas, Oct. 28, 1865, Davis to O. O. Howard, Oct. 27, 30, 1865, M826, reel 10, NA; rough drafts of these letters, Joseph E. Davis Papers, MDAH, and Natchez Trace Collection, University of Texas, Austin.

9. Joseph Davis to President Johnson, Oct. 30, 1865; Joseph Davis Papers, MDAH.

10. Endorsement of President Johnson on letter of W. S. Moore of Vicksburg, Aug. 15, 1865, M826, reel 1, NA; Sharkey to Johnson, wire, Aug. 20, 1865, in Harris, *Presidential Reconstruction,* 72; Davis to Johnson, Oct. 30, 1865, Joseph Davis Papers, MDAH.

11. Montgomery to Davis, Nov. 10, 1865, Joseph E. Davis Papers, MDAH; Special Orders No. 46, BRFAL for State of Mississippi, Oct. 30, 1865, M826, reel 28, NA.

12. Harris, *Presidential Reconstruction,* 12, 87, 128; *Papers,* 2:170, 360, Card of A. Burwell, Nov. 20, 1865, M826, reel 10, NA.

13. Burwell to Davis, Nov. 15, 1865, Natchez Trace Collection, University of Texas, Austin.

14. Davis to Burwell, Nov. 16, 1865, Joseph Davis Papers, MDAH.

15. Card of A. Burwell, Nov. 20, 1865, M826, reel 10, NA.

16. "Notes of testimony taken before the board ordered by Col. Thomas," n.d.; Davis to the Board of Officers, n.d., both in Joseph Davis Papers, MDAH.

17. Report of Investigating Board, Nov. 24, 1865, M826, reel 10, NA.

18. Montgomery to Davis, Nov. 18, 1865, Joseph Davis Papers, MDAH; Stuart Eldridge to Jas. A. Hawley, Nov. 21, 1865, M826, reel 1.

19. Report of Investigating Board, Nov. 24, 1865, M826, reel 10, NA.

20. Thomas to Howard, Nov. 13, 1865, M826, reel 1; Davis to President Andrew Johnson, Jan. 16, 1866, M826, reel 15, NA.

21. J. E. Davis to Andrew Johnson, Nov. 25, 1865, and J. E. Davis to Hon. W. L. Sharkey, Nov. 26, 1865, Hdqs. Off., Land Div., Let. Rcd., D45, BRFAL, RG105, and M826, reel 11, NA.

22. Thomas to Howard, Dec. 22, 1865, M826, reel 1, NA.

23. Thomas to Howard, Dec. 22, 1865, M826, reel 1, NA; C. J. Mitchell to J. E. Davis, Jan. 16, 1866, Lise Mitchell Papers, Tulane University, New Orleans.

24. Joseph Davis to Henry Wilson, Dec. 24, 1865, Joseph E. Davis Papers, MDAH and M826, reel 16, NA.

25. Endorsements on Davis to Wilson, Dec. 24, 1865, and Howard to Davis, Feb. 23, 1866, M826, reel 16, NA; Reg. Let. Rec., Miss. Dept. of, March 13, 1866, with note "Copy of Gen Woods letter furnished to Senator Wilson," April 27, 1866, M752, reel 4, NA; Joseph Davis to O. O. Howard, March 9, 1866, Natchez Trace Collection.

26. Davis to C. J. Mitchell, Feb. 1, 1866; Davis to "His Excellency, the President of the United States," Jan. 28, 1866; Davis to Major General T. J. Wood, Jan. 24, 1866, Natchez Trace Collection.

27. J. E. Davis to Honl. J. Guthrie, Jan. 28, 1866, Headquarters Office, Land Division, Letters Received, BRFAL, RG105, NA.

28. *Vicksburg Journal,* March 8, 1866; J. E. Davis and W. T. Sawyer to President Johnson, Feb. 28, 1866, several drafts, Joseph E. Davis Papers, MDAH.

29. Burton N. Harrison to General Richard Taylor, March 27, 1866, Land Division, Letters Received, BRFAL, RG105, NA; *Natchez Weekly Courier,* April 2, 1866; Hudson Strode, *Jefferson Davis, Tragic Hero* (New York, 1964), 277.

30. Amnesty oath of J. E. Davis, April 21, 1866; N. H. Moulton to President, May 9, 1866, both in File of J. E. Davis, Amnesty Papers, Records of Adjutant General's Office, RG94, NA.

31. Endorsements of Humphreys, Yerger, and Johnston, April 23, 1866, ibid.

32. Endorsements of the president and O. O. Howard on amnesty petition, ibid.

33. File of J. E. Davis, Amnesty Papers, Records of Adjutant General's Office, RG94, NA; Davis to the president, May 9, 1866, Land Division, Letters Received, BRFAL, RG105, NA; T. J. Wood to O. O. Howard, telegram, May 24, 1866, M826, reel 1, NA; Joseph Davis to Hugh R. Davis, April 23, 1866, Museum of the Confederacy, Richmond, Va.

34. Davis to U. S. Grant, July 8, 1866; Davis letter fragment, "For the President," n.d., Natchez Trace Collection.

35. Davis to Wood, Sept. 8, 1866, Land Division, Letters Received, BRFAL, and M826, reel 6, RG105, NA, and Joseph Davis Papers, MDAH; A. M. Preston, Assistant Attorney General, endorsement on above letter, Sept. 11, 1866, Joseph Davis Papers, MDAH; Davis to Andrew Johnson, Aug. 2, 1866, Joseph Davis Papers, MDAH, and Natchez Trace Collection.

36. Drafts of Davis to "The President of U.S.," Sept. 15, 1866, Natchez Trace Collection, University of Texas, Austin, and Joseph E. Davis Papers, MDAH; statements of M. Shannon, F. N. Steele, J. C. Chappell, and A. H. Arthur, Sept. 12, 1866, *Davis* v. *Bowmar,* 540 – 44, MDAH.

37. J. H. D. Bowmar to Joseph E. Davis, Sept. 28, 1866, enclosed in Joseph Davis to C. J. Mitchell, Oct. 11, 1866, Lise Mitchell Papers.

38. Joseph Davis to C. J. Mitchell, Oct. 11, 1866, enclosing J. H. D. Bowmar to Joseph E. Davis, Sept. 28, 1866, ibid.; J. H. D. Bowmar to O. O. Howard, Sept. 26, 1866, Land Division, Letters Received, BRFAL, RG105, NA.

39. Th. J. Wood to O. O. Howard, Oct. 3, 1866, *Senate Executive Document* 6, 39th Cong., 2d sess., 99; Wm. Fowler to T. J. Wood, Oct. 29, 1866, Stuart Eldridge to T. J. Wood, Oct. 17, 1866, M826, reel 16; T. J. Wood to O. O. Howard, Nov. 30, 1866, M752, reel 5, BRFAL, NA.

40. Mortgage recorded in Warren County, Miss., Land Records, Office of Chancery Clerk, Deed Book VV, p. 14, handwritten copy, Joseph Davis Papers, MDAH; Hermann, *Pursuit,* 109 – 11.

41. Jefferson Davis memo, Dec. 17, 1866, Jefferson Davis v.

J. H. D. Bowmar et al., Warren County Chancery Court, July 3, 1874–Jan. 8, 1876, unreported, pp. 586–87, MDAH; Joseph Davis to Jefferson Davis, March 26, 1867, Jefferson Davis Papers, University of Alabama, Tuscaloosa.

42. Harris, *Presidential Reconstruction,* 174–80; the Catchings case papers and those of all other cases mentioned can be found in the Joseph Davis Papers, MDAH.

43. J. W. Payne to Joseph Davis, March 16, 1866, W. C. Van Benthuysen to Joseph E. Davis, Oct. 13, 1866, March 12, 27, Dec. 13, 19, 1867, Jan. 12, Feb. 4, April 4, 1868, Joseph E. Davis Papers, MDAH.

44. Joseph Davis to Jefferson Davis, Aug. 16, 1866, Museum of the Confederacy.

45. Joseph Davis to Jefferson Davis, May 4, 1870, Payne Huntington & Co. to Joseph Davis, April 9, 1870, J. D. Van Benthuysen to J. D. Nicholson, March 27, 1867, J. D. Nicholson to Joseph Davis, Nov. 15, 1867, John Jackson to Joseph Davis, Dec. 10, 1866, Joseph E. Davis Papers, MDAH.

46. Joseph Davis to Hugh R. Davis, April 23, 1866, Museum of the Confederacy; *Papers,* 1 : 275.

47. Jefferson Davis to Lise Mitchell, Oct. 24, 1870, Lise Mitchell to Joseph Davis, Jan. 21, [1866], Lise Mitchell Papers.

48. Jefferson Davis to Lise Mitchell, Nov. 20, 1867, Jefferson Davis Papers, New York Public Library; Rent receipt for $120, Joseph Davis, on First National Bank of Vicksburg, Dec. 6, 1867; Personalty Tax of Joseph E. Davis, Warren County, May 30, 1867; invoice for Havana cigars, Payne Huntington & Co., New Orleans, Jan. 10, 1868, Feb. 11, 1870, Joseph E. Davis Papers, MDAH.

49. Lise Mitchell to Jefferson Davis, Feb. 8, 1870; Jefferson Davis Papers, University of Alabama.

50. J. H. D. Bowmar to Jefferson Davis, Oct. 7, 1870, J. E. Davis to Mrs. James McGill, Aug. 12, 1870, Joseph Davis to Wm. Yerger, July 11, 1870, Payne Huntington & Co. to Joseph Davis, Dec. 28, 1869, Feb. 11, 1870, Colonel C. E. Hooker to Joseph Davis, Jan. 24, 1870, Ben Montgomery to Joseph Davis, April 7, 1870, MDAH; Jefferson Davis to Lise Mitchell, Jan. 14, 1870, Lise Mitchell Papers; Lise Mitchell to Jefferson Davis, Feb. 8, 1870, Jefferson Davis Papers, University of Alabama.

51. *Vicksburg Times,* Sept. 20, 1870.

52. *Weekly Clarion* (Jackson), Sept. 29, 1870. Obituaries were also published in the *Hinds County Gazette* (Raymond), Sept. 28, 1870, and the *Weekly Mississippi Pilot* (Jackson), Sept. 24, 1870.

53. *Papers,* 2:57, 3:56–57; Lise Mitchell Journal; Frank E. Everett, Jr., *Brierfield: Plantation Home of Jefferson Davis* (Hattiesburg, Miss., 1971), 97–105; Davis v. Bowmar, passim, MDAH.

INDEX

Pinckneyville, Mississippi, 19
Pitchford, William, 8, 9
Poindexter, George, 26, 29–30
Polk, Leonidas, 128
Porterfield, Julia Lyons, 66, 120, 136–37, 163
Porterfield, William, 66, 115, 136–37
Postelthwaite, Henry, 37

Quarles, Martha. *See* Harris, Martha Quarles
Quitman, Eliza Turner, 47
Quitman, John A., 46–47, 63–64, 86

Racial attitudes, frontier Georgia, 6–7; Mississippi, 31, 60, 87
Reed, Margaret Ross, 60–61
Reed, Thomas B., 34–35, 41, 60
Religion, Christ Church, Vicksburg, 164; "earthquake Christians," 20; Phillips Mill Baptist Church, Georgia, 5–7; Second Great Awakening begins, 10; and women at Hurricane, 73–74
Robins, Thomas E., 68–69, 87–88, 142
Ross, Isaac, 60–61
Rousseau, Lovell H., 153
Rucks, James T., 160
Russellville, Kentucky, 14–15

Sawyer, W. T., 151
Seymour, Horatio, 152
Shannon, M., 155
Sharkey, James E., 62–63

Sharkey, William L., 134, 141, 146, 148, 150, 156
Shelby, Rachel, 16, 47
Sherman, William T., 124, 128, 130, 134
Sloan, William B., 142
Smith, E. P., 159
Smith, M. L., 105, 106
Stamps, Lucinda Davis, 82
Stamps, Isaac, 101
Stamps, Mary, 101, 103
Stamps, William, 82
Stanton, Edwin M., 155–56
Steamboats, 20–21, 81–82, 102–03
Steedman, James B., 153

Taylor, Richard, 98, 151
Taylor, Zachary, 70, 77–78, 90, 98
Tecumseh, 23
Thomas, Samuel, 139–49
Toulmin, Harry, 28
Trumbull, L. S., 153
Turner, Edward, 35–38, 54, 63

Van Benthuysen, David, 104
Van Benthuysen, Mary, 83
Van Benthuysen, W. C., 160
Van Dorn, Earl, 114, 115
Van Winkle, P. G., 153
Vicksburg, 32, 86–88, 103, 120–22, 135

Wailes, Benjamin L. C., 38
Wallace, William, 14–15, 69
Washington, George, 4, 97
Washington, Georgia, 5

Index